Emerald Apron

Culinary Creations for the Conscious Cook

SAMIN LISA

Samin Lisa

Emerald Apron

Table of Contents

Samin Lisa

Emerald Apron

Book Introduction:

Welcome to *The Green Apron: Plant-Based Made Easy, Simple Steps to Delicious Vegetarian Meals*. In this book, we embark on a journey to explore the vibrant and flavorful world of plant-based cuisine. Whether you are a seasoned vegetarian, a curious omnivore, or simply looking to incorporate more vegetables into your diet, this book is your ultimate guide to creating delicious and satisfying plant-based meals.

The Green Apron represents more than just an apron worn by chefs in the kitchen. It symbolizes a commitment to sustainable and compassionate eating, as well as a celebration of the bountiful offerings of nature. By adopting a plant-based lifestyle, you not only nourish your body with wholesome ingredients but also contribute to the well-being of our planet and its inhabitants.

Plant-based eating is more than just a trend; it is a conscious choice to embrace a healthier and more compassionate way of life. This book aims to empower you with the knowledge, inspiration, and practical tips to make plant-based cooking easy, enjoyable, and accessible to everyone, regardless of culinary expertise or dietary preferences.

In the following chapters, we will delve into the foundations of plant-based eating, equipping you with the essential tools and techniques to create mouthwatering vegetarian meals. We will explore the art of flavoring dishes with a variety of spices, herbs, and sauces, as well as the importance of sourcing fresh and seasonal produce.

You'll discover the versatility of plant-based proteins, from legumes and tofu to tempeh and seitan, and learn how to incorporate them seamlessly into your meals. We will also explore the abundance of grains, legumes, and seeds that form the backbone of a nourishing plant-based diet, providing you with the energy and nutrients you need to thrive.

Throughout this book, you'll find a collection of carefully curated recipes that showcase the diversity and creativity of plant-based cooking. From comforting soups and hearty salads to satisfying main courses and indulgent desserts, there is something for every palate and occasion. Each recipe is accompanied by clear instructions, helpful tips, and nutritional information, ensuring that you can confidently recreate these dishes in your own kitchen.

Beyond the recipes, we will address common challenges and misconceptions associated with plant-based eating. We'll discuss strategies for navigating social situations, dining out, and traveling while maintaining your plant-based lifestyle. Additionally, we'll provide guidance on meal planning, grocery shopping, and stocking your pantry with plant-based essentials.

Whether you are seeking to improve your health, reduce your environmental impact, or explore new culinary horizons, *The Green Apron: Plant-Based Made Easy, Simple Steps to Delicious Vegetarian Meals* is your go-to resource. Let this book be your companion as you embark on a delicious and rewarding journey toward a more vibrant, compassionate, and sustainable way of eating. So, don your green apron and let's get started!

In addition to the incredible health benefits and positive impact on the environment, adopting a plant-based lifestyle is an opportunity to unleash your culinary creativity and discover a world of exciting flavors and textures. *The Green Apron* invites you to step into the kitchen with confidence, knowing that plant-based cooking can be both simple and satisfying.

This book is designed to make plant-based eating easy and accessible for everyone, regardless of your level of culinary expertise. Whether you're a seasoned chef or a novice in the kitchen, the step-by-step instructions and practical tips will empower you to create delicious vegetarian meals with ease. You'll learn essential cooking techniques, such as sautéing, roasting, and grilling, as well as tricks for achieving the perfect balance of flavors in your dishes.

Emerald Apron

The recipes in *The Green Apron* have been carefully crafted to showcase the incredible versatility of plant-based ingredients. From comforting classics to innovative and exciting dishes, you'll find a wide range of options to suit every taste and occasion. Dive into hearty soups and stews that warm the soul, whip up vibrant salads bursting with freshness, and savor satisfying main courses that will leave you feeling nourished and satisfied.

But this book is more than just a cookbook—it's a guide to transforming your entire approach to food. It encourages you to explore new ingredients, experiment with different flavor combinations, and embrace the abundance of plant-based options available to you. With each recipe, you'll develop a deeper appreciation for the incredible flavors and textures that nature provides.

Beyond the kitchen, *The Green Apron* also delves into the broader aspects of a plant-based lifestyle. You'll find practical advice for incorporating plant-based eating into your everyday life, including tips for dining out, traveling, and navigating social situations. The book also addresses common questions and misconceptions surrounding plant-based diets, providing evidence-based information to empower you to make informed choices.

Throughout this journey, you'll discover that *The Green Apron* isso much more than a book —it is representative of a community of like-minded individuals passionate about plant-based living. It encourages you to connect with others who share your values and provide support and inspiration along the way. Whether it's through local meet-ups, online forums, or social media, you'll find a network of individuals ready to share their experiences and offer guidance on your plant-based journey.

As you embark on this culinary adventure with *The Green Apron*, remember that it's not about perfection—it's about progress. Each step you take towards incorporating more plant-based meals into your diet is a step towards a healthier, more sustainable future. By embracing *The Green Apron*, you're joining a movement that has the power to positively impact your well-being, the planet, and future generations.

So, open these pages and let the enticing aromas and vibrant flavors guide you towards a world of delicious vegetarian meals. Get ready to unleash your inner chef, discover new ingredients, and create dishes that will nourish your body and delight your taste buds. *The Green Apron* is your gateway to a fulfilling and satisfying plant-based lifestyle. Let's embark on this transformative journey together, one delectable meal at a time.

Emerald Apron

Chapter 1

Embracing the Green Apron Lifestyle

In this chapter, we will delve into the essence of the Green Apron lifestyle and explore the reasons why embracing a plant-based way of eating can have a transformative impact on your health, the environment, and the well-being of animals.

Embracing a plant-based lifestyle means making a conscious choice to prioritize plant-based foods in your diet while minimizing or eliminating the consumption of animal products. It is about nourishing your body with wholesome ingredients that come directly from nature and aligning your choices with compassion for animals and the planet.

When you adopt the Green Apron lifestyle, you are not just changing your diet; you are fostering a holistic approach to well-being that extends beyond the food on your plate. It involves a shift in mindset, a commitment to mindful eating, and a desire to make a positive difference in the world.

One of the key reasons to embrace the Green Apron lifestyle is the wealth of positive impacts it can have on your health. Plant-based eating has been associated with numerous health benefits. It can help reduce the risk of chronic diseases such as heart disease, type 2 diabetes, and certain types of cancer. A diet rich in fruits, vegetables, whole grains, legumes, nuts, and seeds provides essential nutrients, antioxidants, and fiber that support optimal health and well-being.

Emerald Apron

Not only does the Green Apron lifestyle benefit your personal health, but it also contributes to the well-being of the planet. Animal agriculture is a significant contributor to environmental issues such as deforestation, water pollution, and greenhouse gas emissions. By reducing or eliminating the consumption of animal products, you can reduce your carbon footprint and help mitigate climate change. Plant-based eating is a less intensive practice on agricultural resources, such as land and water, making it a more sustainable choice that supports the preservation of natural ecosystems.

Choosing a plant-based lifestyle is also an ethical choice that reflects compassion for animals. Factory farming and the mass production of animal products often involve practices that compromise animal welfare. By embracing plant-based eating, you can contribute to a more humane and compassionate world. You are making a conscious decision to protect and respect the lives of animals, reducing their suffering and promoting a more ethical approach to food consumption.

Embracing the Green Apron lifestyle is not about deprivation or sacrifice; it is about discovering a world of delicious and nourishing plant-based foods. The abundance of fruits, vegetables, whole grains, legumes, nuts, and seeds offers a wide variety of flavors, textures, and culinary possibilities. It is a journey of culinary exploration, where you can discover new ingredients, experiment with different flavors, and develop your skills in the kitchen.

Transitioning to a plant-based lifestyle may seem daunting at first, but with the right information and resources, it can be a smooth and enjoyable process. Start by educating yourself about plant-based nutrition, understanding the importance of macronutrients and micronutrients, and learning how to create balanced and nutrient-rich meals. Explore new recipes, try different cooking techniques, and you will be amazed at the diversity in the world of plant-based cuisine.

It is important to approach the Green Apron lifestyle with a positive mindset and set realistic goals. The transition does not have to happen overnight. You can start by incorporating more plant-based meals into your diet gradually. Experiment with plant-based substitutes for your favorite animal-based dishes and discover the joy of preparing and enjoying plant-based meals with family and friends.

Building a supportive community is another crucial aspect of embracing the Green Apron lifestyle. Connect with like-minded individuals who share your values and goals. Join local plant-based groups, participate in online forums or social media communities, and attend plant-based events or workshops. Surrounding yourself with a supportive network can provide inspiration, motivation, and valuable resources as you navigate your plant-based journey.

In your Green Apron journey, it's important to develop a deeper understanding of plant-based nutrition. Educate yourself about the essential nutrients found in plant-based foods, such as protein, healthy fats, vitamins, and minerals. You will learn how to create balanced meals that provide all the necessary nutrients your body needs to thrive. By nourishing yourself with a variety of plant-based ingredients, you can enjoy a well-rounded and fulfilling diet.

The Green Apron lifestyle also encourages you to embrace mindful eating. In a fast-paced world where mealtimes become less of a communal ritual and more of an indivual sprint to the finish, the act of eating mindfully can encourage you to slow down, savor each bite, and pay attention to the sensations and flavors of your meals. By practicing mindful eating, you can develop a stronger connection with your food, listen to your body's hunger and fullness cues, and cultivate a healthier relationship with eating.

To fully embrace the Green Apron lifestyle, it's essential to create a kitchen environment that supports your plant-based journey. Stock your pantry with a variety of plant-based staples, including whole grains, legumes, nuts, seeds, herbs, and spices. Having these ingredients readily available will make it easier to whip up delicious and nutritious plant-based meals. Explore local farmers' markets or join a community-supported agriculture (CSA) program to access fresh, seasonal produce that will add vibrancy to your dishes.

Consider incorporating eco-friendly practices into your cooking routine, such as minimizing food waste, composting vegetable scraps, and utilizing reusable containers and bags. By reducing waste and making conscious choices, you can contribute to a more sustainable future.

Emerald Apron

Meal planning plays a crucial role in maintaining a successful Green Apron lifestyle. Take the time to plan your meals in advance, considering your schedule, dietary preferences, and nutritional needs. This practice not only saves you time and energy but also ensures that you have wholesome plant-based meals readily available. A common misconception about plant-based diets is that they are time consuming; this couldn't be further from the truth! Experimenting with batch cooking, preparing larger portions that can be enjoyed throughout the week or frozen for later use is extremely easy to do with plant-based meals. You also don't have the added concern of worrying if you defrosted that chicken correctly! Having a well-thought-out meal plan in place sets you up for success and reduces the likelihood of resorting to less healthy or convenient options.

It's always fun to undertake a new experience with people instead of alone. Seek out like-minded individuals who share your passion for plant-based living. Connect with local plant-based groups, attend cooking classes or workshops, and engage with online communities dedicated to plant-based eating. Sharing experiences, recipe ideas, and challenges with others can provide inspiration, encouragement, and a sense of camaraderie.

Remember, embracing the Green Apron lifestyle is not about perfection but progress. It's about making conscious choices and continuously learning and evolving. Allow yourself the freedom to experiment, try new flavors and ingredients, and adapt recipes to suit your tastes and preferences. Celebrate the small victories along the way and embrace the joy and satisfaction that comes from nourishing yourself and the planet.

Part of embracing the Green Apron lifestyle is also about expanding your culinary horizons and discovering new flavors and ingredients. Plant-based eating opens up a world of possibilities when it comes to creating delicious and satisfying meals. It encourages you to experiment with different fruits, vegetables, grains, legumes, and spices, allowing you to create dishes that are both nourishing and exciting to your taste buds.

As you embark on your Green Apron journey, it's important to remember that there isn't a one-size-fits-all approach. Embrace the flexibility and adaptability of plant-based eating to suit your individual preferences, dietary needs, and cultural influences. Feel free to modify recipes, swap ingredients, and get creative in the kitchen. The understanding that food preparation is not a chore, but a creative endeavour is tantamount to enjoying the fruits of your labour in the kitchen.

One of the keys to successfully embracing the Green Apron lifestyle is to be prepared. Take the time to plan your meals, create shopping lists, and stock up on essential pantry items. By having a well-stocked kitchen, you'll have the necessary ingredients on hand to create delicious plant-based meals whenever inspiration strikes.

In addition to planning your meals, it's helpful to develop your cooking skills and knowledge of plant-based cooking techniques. Experiment with different methods such as sautéing, roasting, steaming, and baking to bring out the best flavors in your ingredients. Learn about flavor profiles, herbs, spices, and seasoning combinations that can elevate your dishes to new heights. Did you know that by using herbs and spices, you won't have to add salt to enhance flavours? Of course, you are free to use salt as you wish, but many people think of salt as the only flavour enhancer, when there are so many more options.

Embracing the Green Apron lifestyle is not just about the food on your plate. It's also about cultivating a positive mindset and a sense of gratitude for the nourishment and abundance that nature provides. Take the time to connect with nature, whether it's through gardening, visiting local farmers' markets, or simply enjoying a walk in the park. Developing a deeper appreciation for the natural world can enhance your relationship with food and further solidify your commitment to a plant-based lifestyle. It is far too easy to become detached from the source of your food when you just see it wrapped in plastic at the supermarket.

Emerald Apron

Meal planning is a practical tool that can support your transition to a plant-based lifestyle. If you take a few hours per week to plan your meals ahead, you can ensure you have a variety of nutritious and delicious options available. Plan your shopping trips accordingly, and consider batch cooking to save time during busy days. Meal planning also helps to minimize food waste, as you can utilize ingredients across multiple dishes throughout the week.

As you navigate your Green Apron journey, it's important to be mindful of your body's unique needs. While a plant-based diet can provide ample nutrition, it's essential to pay attention to specific nutrients that may require additional consideration. For example, make sure you're getting enough vitamin B12, which is primarily found in animal products. Consider incorporating fortified plant-based foods or supplements to meet your needs. If you have specific dietary restrictions or health concerns, it may be beneficial to consult with a registered dietitian or healthcare professional who specializes in plant-based nutrition to ensure you are meeting your nutritional requirements. It is always a good idea to check-in with a dietician before you embark on any food-related journeys.

Section 1: Understanding the Power of Plant-Based Eating

The Benefits of Plant-Based Eating

In this section, we will explore the myriad benefits that come with embracing a plant-based lifestyle. From personal health improvements to environmental sustainability and ethical considerations, understanding the power of plant-based eating will motivate and inspire you on your Green Apron journey.

Personal Health: A plant-based diet has been linked to numerous health benefits. It can help reduce the risk of chronic diseases such as heart disease, type 2 diabetes, and certain types of cancer. It can also lower cholesterol (which is found in red meat), and improve kidney function. When done correctly, a plant-based diet can also reduce the risk of obesity.

Environmental Sustainability: Animal agriculture is a significant contributor to greenhouse gas emissions, deforestation, and water pollution. Cattle contribute a huge amount of methane, a greenhouse gas that exacerbates climate change. Furthermore, cattle farming requires a significant amount of arable land, meaning that biodiversity is greatly reduced and impacted by high numbers of farmed cattle.

Ethical Considerations: The Green Apron lifestyle is rooted in compassion for animals. The mass production of animal products often involves practices that compromise animal welfare. Ever seen videos or documentaries of animal production? To say it's not cruel is a massive understatement. By adopting a plant-based way of eating, you make a conscious choice to minimize the harm inflicted on animals, reducing their suffering and promoting a more compassionate approach to food consumption.

Section 2: The Mindset and Approach of the Green Apron Lifestyle

2.1 Shifting to a Compassionate Mindset
Embracing the Green Apron lifestyle involves cultivating a mindset of compassion. By acknowledging the ethical implications of our dietary choices, we can make more informed decisions that align with our values. In our stressful world, most people are so detached from the food we eat that we can't even find it within ourselves to care how it ended up on our plates. Engaging actively with the production of your food is essential to understanding what you are eating and where it came from.

2.2 Nurturing a Mindful Approach

Mindful eating is an integral part of the Green Apron lifestyle. It involves paying deliberate attention to our food, eating with intention, and savoring each bite. By practicing mindfulness, we become more attuned to our body's hunger and fullness cues, making it easier to maintain a healthy relationship with food. Mindful eating also allows us to fully appreciate the flavors, textures, and nourishment that plant-based meals provide.

Section 3: Practical Considerations for Embracing the Green Apron Lifestyle

Emerald Apron

3.1 Making Informed Food Choices

To embrace the Green Apron lifestyle, it's important to make informed food choices. There are so many ways and resources you can utilize to yourself about plant-based nutrition, including the essential nutrients found in plant-based foods. Ensure you are meeting your nutritional needs by incorporating a variety fruit, nuts and veggies into your diet.

3.2 Discovering Culinary Creativity

Ever heard of celeriac? What about sweet potatoes, jackfruit or sunchoke? There are so many varieties of tasty and unusual vegetables available. They might not be available in your local supermarket-chain, but this is part of the fun! Find small, independent fruit and veggie sellers in your locality, and you can support them while getting to try exciting new flavours.

Section 4: Overcoming Challenges and Navigating Transitions

4.1 Dealing with Social Situations

Transitioning to a plant-based lifestyle may bring about social challenges, especially when dining out or attending social gatherings. What do you do if your uncle wants to go to the local steakhouse for his birthday dinner? It's not always ideal, but if you can, look up a menu's restaurant online before you go, and it should help you to decide if you need to eat before you go. Many restaurants will also happily knock up something vegetarian if you ask nicely!

4.2 Building a Plant-Based Pantry

Stocking a plant-based pantry is a key aspect of the Green Apron lifestyle. Learn about essential ingredients to keep on hand, such as whole grains, legumes, spices, and condiments, to make filling and tasty meals. Experiment with plant-based substitutes for dairy, eggs, and meat to ensure you have versatile options for cooking and baking. Tofu is really tasty and couldn't be easier to prepare – there's a reason why is a vegetarian staple! By having a well-stocked pantry, you'll feel empowered to create delicious plant-based dishes at any time.

4.3 Time and Budget Considerations

Managing time and budget is important when embracing the Green Apron lifestyle. Discover time-saving techniques, such as meal planning, batch cooking, and prepping ingredients in advance. Explore budget-friendly options like buying in bulk, utilizing seasonal produce, and incorporating more affordable plant-based proteins, such as beans and lentils, into your meals. These strategies can help you optimize your resources while enjoying a diverse and satisfying plant-based diet.

Section 5: Cultivating Sustainable Cooking Practices

5.1 Minimizing Food Waste

Reducing food waste is an essential part of the Green Apron lifestyle. Learn how to make the most of your ingredients by utilizing kitchen scraps for homemade vegetable broth, repurposing leftovers into new meals, and practicing portion control to minimize excess food. Composting is another sustainable practice that can turn food scraps into nutrient-rich soil for your garden. By minimizing waste, you contribute to a more sustainable food system.

5.2 Choosing Sustainable Cooking Methods

Explore cooking techniques that maximize flavor while minimizing energy consumption. Opt for methods like steaming, sautéing, roasting, or grilling, which require less oil and use lower heat settings. Consider using energy-efficient appliances and cookware, such as induction stoves or slow cookers, to reduce energy usage. By adopting sustainable cooking practices, you reduce your environmental impact while creating delicious plant-based meals.

Section 6: Embracing a Mindful Approach to Eating

6.1 Mindful Meal Preparation

Emerald Apron

Embracing the Green Apron lifestyle involves more than just eating plant-based foods; it's about being present and mindful throughout the entire process, including meal preparation. Take the time to engage all your senses while cooking, from the vibrant colors of fruits and vegetables to the enticing aromas that fill your kitchen. Embrace the process of chopping, sautéing, and tasting, fully immersing yourself in the act of creating nourishing meals – we know it's easier said than done when you're tired after a hard day's work, but it's worth it.

6.2 Mindful Eating Practices

Mindful eating goes beyond simply choosing plant-based foods; it's about cultivating a deeper connection with your body and the food you consume. Don't hurry to shove all the food in your mouth at once. Chewing carefully can also increase your metabolism and is healthier for your digestive system.

Section 7: Personalizing the Green Apron Lifestyle

7.1 Adapting to Individual Needs and Preferences
The Green Apron lifestyle is highly customizable, allowing you to adapt it to your individual needs, preferences, and cultural influences. Whether you follow a specific dietary plan, have allergies or intolerances, or incorporate cultural traditions into your meals, the Green Apron lifestyle can be tailored to suit your unique circumstances. Seek out recipes, resources, and support that align with your specific requirements to ensure a successful and enjoyable plant-based journey.

7.2 Celebrating Food Diversity

Plant-based eating offers a vast array of flavors and culinary traditions from around the world. Embrace the diversity of plant-based cuisine by exploring global recipes and ingredients. Discover the vibrant spices of Indian cuisine, the hearty flavors of Mediterranean dishes, or the umami-rich flavors of Asian-inspired meals. Celebrate the richness and variety of plant-based foods, allowing your taste buds to embark on a global culinary adventure.

Chapter 1 has provided a comprehensive exploration of embracing the Green Apron lifestyle, covering the benefits of plant-based eating, cultivating a compassionate and mindful approach, addressing practical considerations, and embracing personalization and diversity. By incorporating these principles into your life, you are embarking on a transformative journey that promotes your well-being, supports the environment, and demonstrates compassion for animals.

Emerald Apron

Chapter 2
The Basics of Plant-Based Eating

In Chapter 2, we will explore the fundamentals of plant-based eating, equipping you with the knowledge and tools necessary to embrace this nourishing and sustainable lifestyle. By understanding the basics of plant-based nutrition, building a balanced plate, and exploring essential food groups, you will be empowered to create delicious and well-rounded plant-based meals that support your overall health and well-being.

Understanding Plant-Based Nutrition:

Plant-based nutrition is centered around harnessing the power of plants to provide our bodies with essential nutrients. Plants offer a rich variety of carbohydrates, proteins, healthy fats, vitamins, minerals, and antioxidants that promote optimal health. By incorporating a diverse range of plant-based foods into your diet, you can ensure you receive the nutrients necessary to feel good and live your life.

Carbohydrates: Carbohydrates are the primary source of energy in a plant-based diet. Whole grains, legumes, fruits, and vegetables are excellent sources of complex carbohydrates, providing sustained energy and essential fiber for digestive health. Emphasizing whole, unrefined carbohydrates in your meals is key to maintaining stable blood sugar levels and supporting overall health.

Protein: Contrary to common misconceptions, plant-based diets can easily meet protein requirements. Plant-based protein sources such as legumes (beans, lentils, and chickpeas), tofu, tempeh, seitan, nuts, seeds, and whole grains offer ample protein. Combining different plant-based protein sources throughout the day ensures a complete amino acid profile, supporting muscle growth, repair, and overall body function.

Healthy Fats: Healthy fats are crucial for various bodily functions, including hormone production, brain health, and absorption of fat-soluble vitamins. Plant-based sources of healthy fats include avocados, nuts, seeds, olives, and plant oils like olive oil and coconut oil. These fats provide essential fatty acids and contribute to satiety, heart health, and inflammation reduction.

Vitamins and Minerals: Plant-based diets are abundant in vitamins and minerals necessary for overall health. Fruits, vegetables, whole grains, nuts, and seeds are excellent sources of vitamins A, C, E, and K, as well as various B-vitamins. Dark leafy greens, legumes, and fortified plant-based products are rich in minerals like calcium, iron, zinc, and magnesium. Emphasizing a diverse array of plant-based foods ensures you receive a broad spectrum of vitamins and minerals.

Building a Balanced Plant-Based Plate:
Creating a balanced plate is essential for meeting your nutritional needs on a plant-based diet. By understanding macronutrient balance and incorporating a variety of plant-based foods, you can ensure a well-rounded and satisfying meal.

Macronutrient Balance: Balancing macronutrients involves including an appropriate ratio of carbohydrates, proteins, and fats in your meals. Fill your plate with whole grains (e.g., quinoa, brown rice, whole wheat bread), legumes, and a generous portion of vegetables. Add a source of plant-based protein, such as tofu, tempeh, or beans, and incorporate healthy fats like avocado, nuts, or seeds. This balanced approach ensures a satisfying meal that provides sustained energy and nourishment.

Fiber-Rich Foods: Fiber plays a crucial role in digestive health, weight management, and disease prevention. Fruits, vegetables, whole grains, legumes, and seeds are all rich sources of dietary fiber. Incorporating a variety of fiber-rich foods into your meals promotes satiety, aids in digestion, and supports a healthy gut microbiome. There is increasing research being done globally on the importance of a healthy gut – it's important to look after yours!

Embracing Color and Variety: The vibrant colors found in plant-based foods signify a rich array of nutrients. Embrace the beauty of a colorful plate by incorporating a variety of fruits and vegetables with different hues. Red, orange, green, purple, and yellow produce each offer unique health-promoting compounds, such as antioxidants and phytonutrients. Experiment with seasonal produce to enhance the flavors, textures, and visual appeal of your meals.

Exploring Essential Food Groups:

Plant-based eating encompasses a wide range of food groups that form the foundation of a nourishing and diverse diet. By understanding and incorporating these essential food groups, you can enjoy a wide variety of flavors, textures, and nutritional benefits.

Fruits and Vegetables: Fruits and vegetables are nutritional powerhouses, providing an array of vitamins, minerals, fiber, and antioxidants. Aim to fill half of your plate with a colorful assortment of fruits and vegetables, including leafy greens, cruciferous vegetables, berries, citrus fruits, and more. Explore different cooking methods and incorporate both raw and cooked options to enjoy the full range of their benefits.

Whole Grains: Whole grains are an excellent source of complex carbohydrates, fiber, and various nutrients. Incorporate whole grain options like quinoa, brown rice, oats, barley, whole wheat pasta, and whole grain bread into your meals. These foods provide sustained energy and contribute to heart health, digestive health, and weight management.

Legumes: Legumes, including beans, lentils, and chickpeas, are versatile plant-based protein sources packed with fiber, vitamins, minerals, and antioxidants. Incorporate legumes into your meals through soups, stews, salads, dips, or bean-based patties. They offer an affordable and sustainable protein option while promoting satiety and supporting gut health.

Nuts and Seeds: Nuts and seeds are nutrient-dense foods that offer healthy fats, protein, fiber, vitamins, minerals, and antioxidants. Almonds, walnuts, chia seeds, flaxseeds, pumpkin seeds, and sunflower seeds are just a few examples. Sprinkle them over salads, incorporate them into smoothies or use them as a topping for plant-based yogurts or oatmeal. These small powerhouses provide a wide range of health benefits when consumed in moderation.

Plant-Based Proteins: Plant-based proteins provide essential amino acids and play a crucial role in supporting muscle growth, repair, and overall body function. Legumes such as beans, lentils, and chickpeas are rich sources of protein. Tofu, tempeh, and seitan are versatile plant-based protein options that can be incorporated into various dishes. Nuts, seeds, and whole grains also offer protein, making it easy to meet your protein needs on a plant-based diet.

Plant-Based Calcium Sources: Calcium is an important mineral for maintaining healthy bones and teeth. While dairy products are a common source of calcium, there are plenty of plant-based options available. Dark leafy greens like kale, collard greens, and bok choy, as well as calcium-fortified plant-based milk alternatives and tofu, can provide adequate amounts of calcium in your diet.

Iron-Rich Plant Foods: Iron is essential for carrying oxygen in the blood and supporting overall energy levels. Plant-based sources of iron include legumes, dark leafy greens, whole grains, nuts, and seeds. Pairing these iron-rich foods with vitamin C-rich foods like citrus fruits, bell peppers, and tomatoes can enhance iron absorption.

Omega-3 Fatty Acids: Omega-3 fatty acids are important for heart health and brain function. While fatty fish is a common source of omega-3s, plant-based sources like flaxseeds, chia seeds, hemp seeds, and walnuts can provide these essential fats. Incorporating these foods into your diet can help meet your omega-3 needs.

Vegan Vitamin B12 Sources: Vitamin B12 is primarily found in animal-based products, so it's important for those following a plant-based diet to ensure adequate intake. Fortified plant-based milk alternatives, nutritional yeast, and certain breakfast cereals can be sources of vitamin B12 for vegans. However, it may be necessary to consider a B12 supplement to meet requirements.

Navigating Grocery Shopping: When transitioning to a plant-based diet, it's helpful to know how to navigate the grocery store. Shop the perimeter of the store, where fresh produce, whole grains, and plant-based proteins are typically found. Read ingredient labels to ensure products are free from animal-derived ingredients. Stock your pantry with plant-based staples such as canned beans, whole grains, and spices to make meal preparation easier. Pro-tip – if you can get to the shops early in the morning, you'll be able to get the freshest produce and bigger varieties. Where possible, shop at your local famrer's market or independent grocer.

Eating Out and Social Situations: Eating out and navigating social situations can sometimes pose challenges for plant-based eaters. Research restaurant menus ahead of time, communicate your dietary needs to the server, and be open to customizing menu items. When attending social events, offer to bring a plant-based dish to share, and don't be afraid to educate others about the benefits of plant-based eating in a respectful manner. You'll probably get a lot of questions about plant-based meals, so if you have a dish on hand, you can just say "Here – wanna try some?"

Plant-Based Eating for Children and Families: Plant-based eating can be suitable for children and families, but it's important to ensure adequate nutrition. Consult with a healthcare professional or registered dietitian to address any concerns and ensure all nutrient needs are being met. Encourage children to participate in meal planning and preparation to foster a positive relationship with food. Associating any dietary change with aesthetic reasons could causes low self-esteem and long-term trauma. Eating plant-based is about caring about your body so that it can do its very important job to the best of its ability!

Plant-Based Substitutes: When transitioning to a plant-based diet, it can be helpful to explore plant-based substitutes for commonly consumed animal products. These substitutes offer similar flavors and textures, allowing you to recreate familiar dishes in a plant-based way. For example, tofu, aubergine, eggplant or tempeh can be used as a substitute for meat in stir-fries or sandwiches, while plant-based milk alternatives like almond milk or oat milk can be used in place of dairy milk.

Gut Health and Fermented Foods: Gut health plays a crucial role in overall well-being, and incorporating fermented foods into your plant-based diet can support a healthy gut microbiome. Fermented foods like sauerkraut, unsweetened natural yoghurt, kimchi, miso, and tempeh contain beneficial probiotics that promote gut health. These foods can enhance digestion, support immune function, and contribute to overall gut balance.

Hydration and Fluid Intake: Staying hydrated is important for overall health and well-being. While water is the primary source of hydration, plant-based foods like fruits and vegetables also contribute to your fluid intake due to their high water content. Aim to drink an adequate amount of water throughout the day and include hydrating foods in your meals and snacks.

Supplementation: While a well-planned plant-based diet can provide all the necessary nutrients, certain individuals may benefit from supplementation. Vitamin B12, as previously mentioned, is a common supplement for those following a plant-based diet. Additionally, individuals who have limited sun exposure may need to consider vitamin D supplementation. People who are menstruating may need to look at taking iron supplements to ensure they do not become anemic.

Long-Term Success and Mindset: Long-term success in plant-based eating is influenced by your mindset and approach. Embrace a positive and flexible mindset, focusing on the abundance and deliciousness of plant-based foods rather than restrictive thinking. Be open to trying new recipes, flavors, and cuisines, and don't be discouraged by occasional slip-ups or deviations from your plant-based eating plan. Remember that progress is more important than perfection, and each plant-based meal you enjoy contributes to your overall health and well-being. This isn't a diet, this is a lifestyle!

Plant-Based Eating for Athletes: Plant-based eating can support athletic performance and recovery. Many athletes have successfully adopted plant-based diets, showcasing enhanced endurance, improved recovery, and reduced inflammation. By ensuring sufficient calorie intake, incorporating a variety of plant-based protein sources, and focusing on nutrient timing, athletes can meet their nutritional needs while thriving on a plant-based diet.

Plant-Based Eating on a Budget: Eating plant-based can be budget-friendly with some research and planning.

Understanding Food Labels: Reading and understanding food labels is important when following a plant-based diet. Look for products that are explicitly labeled as vegan or plant-based. Be aware of hidden animal-derived ingredients such as gelatin, dairy, or honey. Familiarize yourself with commonly used food additives and their plant-based or animal-based sources. Understanding food labels empowers you to make informed choices and align your purchases with your dietary preferences.

Next Chapter Preview:

In the upcoming chapters, we will explore the culinary techniques you can to use to create the flavors of various cuisines, providing a wide range of plant-based recipes that will inspire your cooking creativity. We will cover topics such as plant-based breakfast ideas, satisfying plant-based lunches and dinners, plant-based snacks and desserts, and even tips for entertaining guests with plant-based meals. Get ready to expand your culinary horizons and savor the deliciousness of plant-based eating in the chapters to come.

Plant-Based Snacking: Snacking can be an enjoyable and satisfying part of a plant-based diet. Explore a variety of plant-based snacks such as fresh fruits, raw vegetables with dips like hummus or guacamole, homemade energy bars, roasted chickpeas, or mixed nuts and seeds. These snacks provide a boost of energy and essential nutrients between meals.

Plant-Based Desserts: Yes, not only is making delivious plant-based sweet treats possible – it's easy! Discover plant-based alternatives to classic desserts such as dairy-free ice creams, vegan brownies, fruit crisps, chia seed puddings, or vegan cheesecakes. Experiment with natural sweeteners like dates, maple syrup, or coconut sugar and coconut cream to satisfy your sweet tooth.

Plant-Based Travel and Eating Out: Traveling or eating out while following a plant-based diet can be an exciting adventure. Research local plant-based options and restaurants in your destination ahead of time. Carry portable snacks for travel, and when dining out, clearly communicate your dietary preferences to the restaurant staff. With a little planning and flexibility, you can enjoy delicious plant-based meals wherever your journey takes you.

Plant-Based Eating for Special Dietary Needs: Plant-based eating can be adapted to accommodate various dietary needs or restrictions. Whether you follow a gluten-free, nut-free, or soy-free diet, or have specific allergies or intolerances, there are still plenty of plant-based options available. Discover alternative ingredients and substitutions that meet your specific dietary requirements while still enjoying a diverse and flavorful plant-based diet.

Family and Plant-Based Eating: Transitioning your family to a plant-based lifestyle can be a rewarding and health-promoting choice. Involve your family in meal planning and preparation, and gradually introduce new plant-based foods and flavors. Educate children about the benefits of plant-based eating, and make meals fun and interactive by engaging them in cooking activities. Plant-based eating can be a wonderful opportunity to instill healthy habits and a love for nutritious food in your children.

Samin Lisa

Emerald Apron

Chapter 3

Stocking Your Plant-Based Pantry

In Chapter 3, we will explore the essentials of stocking your plant-based pantry. A plentiful pantry forms the foundation for creating tasty and nutritious plant-based meals. By having a variety of staple ingredients on hand, you'll be prepared to whip up flavorful dishes and experiment with different culinary creations. Let's dive into the key components of a plant-based pantry and discover the versatile ingredients that will elevate your plant-based cooking.

Grains and Flours:
Grains are a staple in plant-based cooking, providing carbohydrates, fiber, and essential nutrients. Stock your pantry with a variety of whole grains like quinoa, brown rice, bulgur, farro, oats, cous-cous and whole wheat pasta. These grains can be used as the base for hearty salads, grain bowls, stir-fries, or side dishes.

In addition to whole grains, keep an assortment of flours on hand. Whole wheat flour, almond flour, coconut flour, and chickpea flour are versatile options that can be used for baking, creating plant-based pancakes, or making gluten-free alternatives.

Legumes and Pulses:
Legumes and pulses are excellent sources of plant-based protein, fiber, and essential nutrients. Stock up on canned or dried legumes such as chickpeas, lentils, black beans, kidney beans, and white beans. They can be transformed into savory dishes like curries, stews, chilis, or used as a base for homemade plant-based burgers and falafels. They keep you full for a long time and are usually cheap to buy at the store.

Nuts, Seeds, and Nut Butters:

Nuts and seeds add texture, flavor, and nutrition to plant-based meals. Keep a variety of nuts such as almonds, walnuts, cashews, and pecans, as well as seeds like chia seeds, flaxseeds, sesame seeds, and pumpkin seeds. These ingredients can be used for toppings, added to salads, incorporated into homemade granola or energy bars, or blended into creamy nut butters.

Plant-Based Milks and Yogurts:
Plant-based milks and yogurts are versatile dairy alternatives that can be used in both sweet and savory recipes. Stock your pantry with options like almond milk, soy milk, oat milk, coconut milk, or rice milk. These alternatives can be used for baking, making creamy sauces, adding to smoothies, or enjoying with granola and fresh fruits. Similarly, plant-based yogurts made from coconut, almond, or soy can be enjoyed as a snack or used in dressings, dips, or desserts.
Condiments and Sauces:
Flavorful condiments and sauces are essential for adding depth and complexity to plant-based dishes. Keep a variety of options like soy sauce, tamari, miso paste, tahini, nutritional yeast, hot sauce, mustard, and vinegars (such as balsamic, apple cider, and rice vinegar). These condiments can be used for marinades, dressings, sauces, and seasoning dishes to enhance their taste profiles.

Herbs, Spices, and Seasonings:
Herbs, spices, and seasonings are the backbone of plant-based cooking, adding aroma, flavor, and depth to your dishes. Stock your pantry with a range of options such as basil, thyme, oregano, rosemary, cumin, paprika, turmeric, cinnamon, ginger, and garlic powder. Experiment with different combinations to create unique and enticing flavors in your plant-based meals.

Oils and Cooking Fats:
Having a selection of cooking oils and fats is essential for sautéing, roasting, and baking. Extra-virgin olive oil, rapeseed oil, peanut oil, avocado oil, coconut oil, and sesame oil are versatile options that can be used for different cooking purposes. Additionally, keep vegan butter or margarine on hand for baking and spreading on toast. Good quality oils are much better for reducing cholesterol than using butter.

Sweeteners:

Plant-based sweeteners are a healthier alternative to refined sugars. Stock your pantry with natural sweeteners like maple syrup, agave nectar, coconut sugar, or dates. These can be used to add sweetness to baked goods, smoothies, dressings, or homemade sauces.

Canned and Jarred Goods:
Canned and jarred goods provide convenience and versatility in plant-based cooking. Keep items like diced tomatoes, tomato paste, coconut milk, vegetable broth, capers, olives, pickles, and jarred sauces (such as salsa or marinara sauce) stocked in your pantry. These ingredients can be used as the base for sauces, soups, stews, or added to grain dishes for extra flavor.

Whole Food Snacks:
Having wholesome snacks on hand is essential for satisfying cravings and providing nourishment between meals. Keep a variety of whole food snacks such as dried fruits, raw nuts, trail mix, rice cakes, popcorn, or energy bars. These snacks can be enjoyed on-the-go or when you need a quick pick-me-up.

Whole Grain Baking Ingredients:
If you enjoy baking, stock your pantry with whole grain baking ingredients. Whole wheat flour, oat flour, almond flour, coconut flour, and baking essentials like baking powder, baking soda, and yeast will allow you to create a variety of delicious and wholesome plant-based baked goods. These ingredients can be used to make bread, muffins, cookies, pancakes, and more.

Dried Herbs and Spices:
Expand your collection of herbs and spices with dried varieties. Dried herbs like thyme, rosemary, basil, parsley, and dill can be used when fresh herbs are not available. Additionally, stock up on dried spices such as chili powder, curry powder, garam masala, coriander, and cayenne pepper. These dried herbs and spices have a longer shelf life and are perfect for adding flavor to your dishes.

Nutritional Yeast:

Nutritional yeast is a staple in plant-based cooking, known for its cheesy and nutty flavor. It is a deactivated yeast that is packed with vitamins, minerals, and protein. Nutritional yeast can be sprinkled on popcorn, pasta, or salads, or used as a flavor enhancer in sauces, dressings, and dips. It adds a rich umami taste to plant-based dishes.

Plant-Based Protein Powders:
Plant-based protein powders are convenient options for supplementing your protein intake, especially for those with higher protein needs or active lifestyles. Choose from a variety of plant-based protein powders like pea, hemp, rice, or soy protein. These powders can be added to smoothies, baked goods, or used to make protein-rich snacks like energy balls.

Fermented Foods:
Include fermented foods in your pantry to promote gut health and add unique flavors to your meals. Options like sauerkraut, kimchi, miso paste, and kombucha are rich in probiotics that support a healthy gut microbiome. Fermented foods not only provide health benefits for your gut biome, but also bring tangy and savory elements to your plant-based dishes.

Specialty Ingredients:
Consider adding some specialty ingredients to your plant-based pantry to enhance the variety and versatility of your meals. These could include ingredients like nutritional powders (maca, spirulina, or acai powder), seaweed (nori sheets or kelp noodles), specialty grains (wild rice, amaranth, or quinoa), or unique plant-based condiments (umeboshi plum paste, tamari soy sauce, or tahini).

Fresh Produce:
While this chapter focuses mainly on pantry staples, it's important to remember the significance of fresh produce in a plant-based diet. Keep a variety of fruits and vegetables in your refrigerator and replenish them regularly. Incorporate seasonal produce for optimal flavor and nutrition. Fresh produce is essential for creating vibrant salads, smoothies, roasted vegetable dishes, and more.

Plant-Based Dairy Alternatives:

In addition to plant-based milks and yogurts, stock your pantry with other dairy alternatives to suit your preferences and culinary needs. Plant-based cheeses made from nuts or soy can add a delightful creamy and cheesy element to your dishes. Non-dairy butter substitutes like the oils mentioned earlier can be used for spreading on bread or in baking. Experiment with different brands and types to find the ones that best suit your taste and texture preferences.

Plant-Based Protein Alternatives:

If you're looking to incorporate more plant-based protein options into your diet, stock your pantry with plant-based protein alternatives. These could include seitan, tempeh, tofu, or plant-based protein powders. These alternatives provide different textures and can be used in various dishes like stir-fries, salads, sandwiches, or as the base for plant-based meat alternatives.

Sweet and Savory Condiments:

To enhance the flavors of your plant-based dishes, keep a variety of sweet and savory condiments in your pantry. Sweet condiments like maple syrup, agave nectar, and date syrup can be used for sweetness in baked goods, dressings, or as a topping for pancakes or waffles. Savory condiments like tamari, mustard, hot sauce, or vegan Worcestershire sauce can add a burst of umami and tang to your savory creations.

Plant-Based Protein Bars and Snacks:

For convenient and on-the-go plant-based snacking, include a selection of plant-based protein bars and snacks in your pantry. Look for options made with whole food ingredients, such as nuts, seeds, and dried fruits, and free from artificial additives. These bars and snacks can provide a quick energy boost and satiate your hunger between meals.

Plant-Based Broths and Stocks:

For flavoring soups, stews, or sauces, keep plant-based broths or stocks in your pantry. Look for options made from vegetable sources, free from animal products. These broths and stocks provide a rich base for adding depth and complexity to your plant-based recipes.

Specialty Grains and Pasta:

Emerald Apron

To add variety to your plant-based meals, consider incorporating specialty grains and pasta into your pantry. Quinoa, wild rice, amaranth, buckwheat, or spelt pasta are just a few examples of grains and pasta that can elevate your dishes with unique textures and flavors.

Dried Fruits and Berries:

Dried fruits and berries are excellent pantry staples for adding natural sweetness and texture to your plant-based meals. Stock up on dried fruits like raisins, dates, cranberries, apricots, or figs. These can be enjoyed as a snack, added to trail mixes, used in baking, or incorporated into savory dishes like grain salads or tagines.

Vinegars and Citrus Juices:

Vinegars and citrus juices are essential for adding acidity and brightness to your plant-based dishes. Keep a variety of vinegars such as balsamic, apple cider, rice, or white wine vinegar. These can be used for dressings, marinades, or to balance flavors in savory recipes. Fresh citrus juices like lemon, lime, or orange juice can also add a refreshing tang to your dishes.

Plant-Based Canned Proteins:

In addition to dried legumes, it can be convenient to have canned plant-based protein options in your pantry. Look for canned chickpeas, black beans, lentils, or mixed beans. These can be quickly incorporated into salads, soups, or pasta dishes, providing a protein boost to your meals.

Plant-Based Sweeteners:

Expand your sweetener options beyond traditional sugars by including a variety of plant-based sweeteners in your pantry. Along with maple syrup, agave nectar, and coconut sugar, consider alternatives like blackstrap molasses, brown rice syrup, or stevia. These sweeteners can be used in baking, smoothies, dressings, or to sweeten beverages.

Plant-Based Bouillon or Seasoning Powders:

For quick and easy flavor enhancement, keep plant-based bouillon cubes or seasoning powders in your pantry. These products can be dissolved in hot water to create a flavorful base for soups, stews, or sauces. Look for options that are free from animal products and made from natural ingredients.

Nutritional Powders and Superfoods:

To boost the nutritional profile of your plant-based meals, consider incorporating nutritional powders and superfoods into your pantry. These can include powders such as spirulina, wheatgrass, maca, or matcha green tea. Superfoods like chia seeds, hemp seeds, goji berries, or acai berries are also great additions. These ingredients can be added to smoothies, oatmeal, energy balls, or used as toppings for salads and desserts.

Plant-Based Salad Dressings and Sauces:
Having a selection of plant-based salad dressings and sauces in your pantry makes it easy to create delicious and flavorful salads, stir-fries, or grain bowls. Look for options that are free from animal products and made with wholesome ingredients. Tahini, tamari-based dressings, vinaigrettes, or vegan mayonnaise are versatile choices that can elevate your dishes.

Plant-Based Condiments:
To add a burst of flavor to your plant-based meals, keep a variety of plant-based condiments in your pantry. These could include mustard, ketchup, vegan mayonnaise, hot sauce, pickles, capers, or soy sauce. These condiments can be used for sandwich spreads, burger toppings, marinades, or as dipping sauces.

When stocking your plant-based pantry, it's important to consider the quality and sourcing of your ingredients. Whenever possible, choose organic options to minimize exposure to pesticides and ensure that your food is produced using sustainable practices. Look for non-GMO products to support biodiversity and avoid genetically modified organisms. Additionally, opt for minimally processed foods that retain their natural nutrients and flavors.

Another aspect to consider is sustainability. Incorporating a variety of whole grains, legumes, and seasonal fruits and vegetables can reduce the environmental impact of your diet. By supporting local farmers and buying locally sourced products, you can reduce the carbon footprint associated with transportation. Furthermore, aim to reduce food waste by properly storing ingredients, utilizing leftovers, and composting organic scraps.

Emerald Apron

Samin Lisa

Chapter 4

Essential Cooking Techniques for Plant-Based Cuisine

In Chapter 4, we delve into the essential cooking techniques that will empower you to create delicious and satisfying plant-based meals. Cooking techniques play a vital role in transforming raw ingredients into flavorful dishes, unlocking the natural tastes and textures of plant-based foods. By mastering these techniques, you'll be able to elevate your culinary skills and bring out the best in every ingredient. Let's explore the fundamental cooking techniques that will take your plant-based cooking to new heights.

Sautéing:
Sautéing is a versatile cooking technique that involves cooking food quickly in a small amount of oil or cooking spray over medium to high heat. It's a great way to bring out the natural flavors and textures of vegetables, tofu, tempeh, or seitan. Start by heating the oil in a skillet or sauté pan, then add your ingredients and cook them until they're tender and slightly browned. Sautéed vegetables can be enjoyed on their own, used as a filling for wraps or sandwiches, or added to stir-fries, pasta dishes, or grain bowls.

Roasting:

Roasting is a technique that adds depth and intensity of flavor to vegetables, fruits, and even plant-based proteins. To roast, preheat your oven to a high temperature (usually around 400°F or 200°C), place the ingredients on a baking sheet, and roast them until they're golden brown and caramelized. Roasting brings out the natural sweetness and creates a slightly crispy exterior, resulting in deliciously tender and flavorful dishes. Roasted vegetables can be enjoyed as a side dish, tossed into salads, or used as a topping for grain bowls or pasta. Roasting vegetables as opposed to boiling them also ensures the vegetables retain more of their nutrients – as well as being a delicious way to cook veggies!

Steaming:
Steaming is a gentle cooking technique that retains the natural flavors, colors, and nutrients of plant-based ingredients. It involves using steam to cook food, usually by placing it in a steamer basket or steaming tray over simmering water. Steamed vegetables, tofu, or tempeh retain their vibrant colors and delicate textures. Steaming is an excellent method for cooking vegetables that are best enjoyed with a slight crunch, such as broccoli, cauliflower, or snap peas. It's also a great way to cook grains like quinoa or rice.

Boiling:
Boiling is a common cooking technique that involves cooking food in a liquid at a temperature where bubbles consistently break the surface. It's often used for cooking grains, legumes, pasta, or potatoes. Boiling allows these ingredients to become tender and fully cooked. To boil, place the food in a pot with enough liquid to cover it and bring it to a boil. Reduce the heat to a simmer and continue cooking until the food reaches the desired tenderness. Boiled grains can be used as a base for salads, pilafs, or served as a side dish, while boiled legumes can be incorporated into soups, stews, or added to salads. Make sure that you don't overboil your food – no one likes a soggy vegetable!

Stir-Frying:

Emerald Apron

Stir-frying is a quick and vibrant cooking technique that originated in Asian cuisine. It involves cooking bite-sized pieces of ingredients, such as vegetables, tofu, or tempeh, in a hot pan or wok with a small amount of oil. The high heat and constant stirring result in tender-crisp vegetables and a beautifully caramelized exterior. Stir-frying allows you to create flavorful and colorful dishes, often seasoned with soy sauce, ginger, garlic, and other aromatic ingredients. Stir-fries can be served over rice or noodles, or enjoyed as standalone dishes.

Baking:

Baking is a versatile cooking technique that allows you to create a wide variety of plant-based dishes, including bread, muffins, cakes, and desserts. Baking involves cooking food in an enclosed space, usually an oven, using dry heat. It's important to preheat the oven to the specified temperature and carefully follow baking recipes to achieve the desired results. Baking requires precise measurements, proper mixing techniques, and attention to baking times to ensure that your plant-based creations are moist, fluffy, and perfectly baked.

Grilling:

Grilling is a popular cooking technique that imparts a smoky and charred flavor to plant-based ingredients. It's a great way to add depth and complexity to vegetables, tofu, tempeh, or plant-based burgers. Grilling can be done using a traditional outdoor grill or an indoor grill pan. Before grilling, marinate your ingredients to enhance their flavors and prevent them from sticking to the grill. Brushing the grill with oil or using a non-stick cooking spray can also help prevent sticking. Grilled vegetables can be enjoyed as a side dish, added to salads, or used as toppings for sandwiches and wraps.

Blending:

Blending is a versatile technique used to create smooth and creamy textures in plant-based cooking. It's commonly used to make smoothies, soups, sauces, dressings, and dips. Blenders or food processors are used to combine ingredients until they reach a smooth and homogeneous consistency. The possibilities are endless when it comes to blending; experiment with different flavor combinations, textures, and ingredient ratios to create your desired results. Blending allows you to incorporate a variety of fruits, vegetables, nuts, seeds, and plant-based milks into your recipes, providing a rich and satisfying experience.

Fermenting:
Fermenting is a unique cooking technique that involves using microorganisms to transform ingredients, typically to enhance their flavor, texture, and nutritional value. Fermentation can be applied to plant-based foods such as kimchi, sauerkraut, pickles, or kombucha. During the fermentation process, beneficial bacteria or yeasts break down sugars and convert them into acids, creating tangy and complex flavors. Fermented foods are not only delicious but also provide probiotics that promote a healthy gut microbiome.

Simmering:
Simmering is a gentle cooking technique that involves cooking food slowly in a liquid at a low temperature. It's commonly used for making soups, stews, sauces, or braising vegetables, tofu, or plant-based proteins. To simmer, place the ingredients in a pot with enough liquid to cover them, then bring the liquid to a boil. Once it reaches a boil, reduce the heat to low, so the liquid maintains a gentle simmer. Simmering allows flavors to meld together and ingredients to become tender and infused with the liquid's essence.

Mashing:
Mashing is a technique used to transform ingredients into a smooth and creamy texture. It's commonly used for mashing potatoes, sweet potatoes, or legumes like chickpeas or beans. Mashing can be done using a potato masher, fork, or food processor. It's a simple yet effective method for creating comforting dishes like mashed potatoes, hummus, or bean dips. Experiment with different spices, herbs, and seasonings to add flavor and depth to your mashed creations.

Blanching:
Blanching is a cooking technique that involves briefly boiling vegetables, then rapidly cooling them in ice water to stop the cooking process. This technique helps retain the vibrant colors and crisp textures of vegetables while partially cooking them. Blanching is often used for preparing vegetables for stir-fries, salads, or freezing. To blanch, bring a pot of water to a boil, add the vegetables, and cook them for a short time. Then, transfer them to a bowl of ice water to cool. Blanching helps preserve the nutritional value of vegetables while maintaining their freshness.

Caramelizing:
Caramelizing is a technique used to bring out the natural sugars in vegetables, resulting in a rich, sweet, and slightly caramelized flavor. It's commonly used for onions, carrots, or root vegetables. To caramelize, sauté the vegetables in a small amount of oil over medium to low heat until they become golden brown and develop a sweet aroma. The slow and low cooking process allows the natural sugars to release and caramelize, creating depth and complexity of flavor. Caramelized vegetables can be used as a side dish, added to grain bowls, or incorporated into various recipes to enhance their taste.

Marinating:
Marinating is a technique used to infuse flavors into plant-based proteins, vegetables, or tofu. It involves soaking the ingredients in a flavorful liquid, usually a mixture of herbs, spices, acids (like citrus juice or vinegar), and oil. Marinating helps tenderize ingredients and enhances their taste. The longer the marination time, the more intense the flavors become. Marinated ingredients can be grilled, sautéed, or baked to retain the delicious flavors infused during the marinating process.

Poaching:
Poaching is a gentle cooking technique that involves cooking food in liquid at a low temperature, just below the boiling point. It's often used for delicate ingredients like tofu, fruits, or vegetables. Poaching helps retain the natural flavors and textures of the ingredients while infusing them with the flavors of the poaching liquid. To poach, place the ingredients in a simmering liquid and cook until they become tender. Poached tofu can be used in salads, sandwiches, or served as a main dish, while poached fruits can be enjoyed on their own or used in desserts.

Breading and Frying:
Breading and frying is a technique that adds a crispy coating to plant-based ingredients like tofu, vegetables, or plant-based "meats." It involves coating the ingredient with a seasoned flour or breadcrumb mixture and then frying it until golden brown and crispy. This technique can be used to create delicious plant-based versions of classic dishes like fried "chicken," crispy tofu, or vegetable tempura. To achieve a lighter and healthier result, consider baking or air frying instead of deep-frying.

Pickling:
Pickling is a technique used to preserve and enhance the flavor of fruits, vegetables, or even spices. It involves immersing the ingredients in a solution of vinegar, water, salt, and spices. The pickling process adds tanginess and complexity to the ingredient while extending its shelf life. Pickled vegetables like cucumbers, carrots, or radishes can be enjoyed as a condiment, added to salads, or used as a topping for sandwiches and burgers. Experiment with different flavors and spices to create your unique pickling combinations.

Grating and Shredding:
Grating and shredding are techniques used to transform ingredients into fine, small pieces. These techniques are commonly used for vegetables like carrots, zucchini, or cabbage. Grated or shredded vegetables can be incorporated into salads, slaws, stir-fries, or used as fillings for wraps or sandwiches. They add texture, color, and a refreshing crunch to your plant-based dishes. A box grater or a food processor with a grating or shredding attachment can be used to achieve the desired results.

Dehydrating:
Dehydrating is a technique used to remove moisture from fruits, vegetables, or herbs, resulting in a concentrated and preserved form. It can be achieved using a dehydrator or an oven set to a low temperature. Dehydrated ingredients can be used in various ways, such as creating dried fruit snacks, making homemade veggie chips, or using dried herbs for seasoning. Dehydrating helps extend the shelf life of ingredients and intensifies their flavors.

Charring:
Charring is a technique that involves exposing ingredients to high heat until they develop a charred or slightly burnt exterior. This technique adds a smoky and complex flavor to vegetables, peppers, or even fruits. Charring can be done using a grill, stovetop burner, broiler, or even a blowtorch for precise control. Charred vegetables can be used in salads, dips, salsas, or as a topping for pizzas or tacos. The charred flavor adds depth and uniqueness to your plant-based creations.

Sprouting:

Sprouting is a technique used to cultivate sprouts from seeds, legumes, or grains. It involves soaking the seeds or legumes in water, then rinsing and draining them regularly until they sprout. Sprouts are packed with nutrients, enzymes, and antioxidants, making them a nutritious addition to salads, sandwiches, wraps, or even smoothies. They add freshness, crunch, and a vibrant touch to your plant-based dishes.

Reduction:
Reduction is a technique used to intensify the flavors of sauces, dressings, or glazes by simmering them until the liquid evaporates and the mixture thickens. It involves cooking the ingredients over low heat for a prolonged period, allowing the flavors to concentrate. Reductions can be made from vegetable broth, fruit juices, vinegars, or other flavorful liquids. The reduced sauces can be drizzled over dishes to add richness and depth.

Infusing:
Infusing is a technique used to extract the flavors of herbs, spices, or aromatics into a liquid medium like oil, vinegar, or plant-based milk. It involves steeping the ingredients in the liquid for a specific period, allowing the flavors to infuse. Infused oils can be used for dressings, marinades, or sautéing, while infused vinegars can be used for dressings or pickling. Infusing adds complexity and depth to your plant-based recipes.

Tempering:
Tempering is a technique commonly used for working with chocolate or creating creamy plant-based desserts. It involves carefully melting and cooling chocolate to achieve a smooth and glossy texture. By following specific temperature guidelines, you can control the crystallization process of the chocolate, resulting in a finished product with a satisfying snap and sheen. Tempering is essential for making chocolate bars, truffles, or coating fruits and nuts.

Braising:

Braising is a slow-cooking technique that involves searing ingredients in a hot pan and then cooking them in a liquid over low heat for an extended period. It's often used for tough cuts of plant-based proteins or hearty vegetables. Braising tenderizes the ingredients while infusing them with rich flavors from the cooking liquid. The slow cooking process results in tender, melt-in-your-mouth dishes. Braised plant-based proteins, such as seitan or tempeh, can be served as main courses, while braised vegetables can be used in stews, curries, or as standalone dishes.

Emulsifying:

Emulsifying is a technique used to create stable mixtures of two immiscible ingredients, such as oil and water. It's commonly used for making creamy dressings, sauces, or mayonnaise. The key to emulsification is gradually incorporating one ingredient into the other while continuously mixing or whisking. The process breaks the ingredients into tiny droplets, allowing them to suspend and create a smooth, homogeneous mixture. Emulsified sauces and dressings can elevate the flavor of your plant-based meals, adding creaminess and richness.

Sous Vide:

Sous vide, meaning "under vacuum" in French, is a precise cooking technique that involves sealing ingredients in a vacuum-sealed bag and cooking them in a temperature-controlled water bath. This method allows for precise temperature control, ensuring that the food is cooked evenly and retains its moisture and flavors. Sous vide is particularly useful for cooking plant-based proteins like tofu or vegetables, resulting in tender and perfectly cooked dishes. It's a technique that requires specific equipment, such as a sous vide machine, to maintain the precise cooking temperature.

Grating and Zesting:

Grating and zesting are techniques used to extract the flavors and aromas from the outer peel of fruits like lemons, limes, or oranges. By using a fine grater or a zester, you can scrape the peel to collect the fragrant oils and finely grated zest. The zest adds bright and citrusy notes to your plant-based dishes, desserts, dressings, or beverages. It's important to grate or zest only the colored part of the peel, avoiding the bitter white pith underneath.

Folding:
Folding is a gentle mixing technique used to incorporate delicate ingredients into a batter or mixture without deflating or overmixing them. It's commonly used for incorporating whipped aquafaba (chickpea brine) or whipped coconut cream into desserts, such as mousse or cake batters. To fold, use a spatula or whisk and gently combine the ingredients by using a gentle folding motion. The goal is to maintain the airiness and volume of the whipped component while ensuring that all ingredients are evenly combined.

Grinding:
Grinding is a technique used to reduce solid ingredients into finer particles or powders. It's commonly used for spices, nuts, seeds, or grains. Grinding can be done using a mortar and pestle, a spice grinder, or a food processor. By grinding ingredients, you release their essential oils and intensify their flavors. Ground spices can be used to season dishes, while ground nuts or seeds can be incorporated into baked goods, sauces, or spreads.

Basting:
Basting is a technique used to keep food moist and add flavor during the cooking process. It involves periodically brushing or spooning liquid, such as marinades, sauces, or melted butter, over the surface of the food while it cooks. Basting helps enhance the flavors, prevent drying out, and create a delicious glaze. It's commonly used for roasted vegetables, plant-based proteins, or even fruits like grilled peaches. Basting can be done using a basting brush or a spoon, ensuring that the liquid is evenly distributed.

Double Boiling:
Double boiling is a gentle cooking technique used for ingredients that are heat-sensitive or require slow and even heating. It involves placing a heat-resistant bowl or a smaller pot inside a larger pot filled with simmering water. The indirect heat gently cooks the ingredients without exposing them to direct heat. Double boiling is commonly used for melting chocolate, making delicate sauces, or tempering ingredients. This technique ensures that the ingredients are heated slowly and evenly, preventing them from scorching or curdling.

Smoking:
Smoking is a technique used to impart a smoky flavor to plant-based ingredients. It involves exposing the ingredients to smoke produced by burning wood chips or other smoking agents. Smoking can be done using a dedicated smoker, stovetop smoker, or even by creating a makeshift smoker using a grill. The smoky flavors add depth and complexity to plant-based proteins, vegetables, or even homemade plant-based cheeses. Experiment with different wood chips and smoking agents to achieve your desired smoky flavors.

Pressure Cooking:
Pressure cooking is a technique that uses high-pressure steam to cook food quickly. It's a convenient method for preparing plant-based meals in a fraction of the time compared to traditional cooking methods. Pressure cookers create a sealed environment, allowing the pressure to build and raise the boiling point of water, resulting in faster cooking times. This technique is ideal for cooking grains, legumes, stews, or soups, as it helps to soften tough ingredients and infuse flavors efficiently.

Chilling and Setting:
Chilling and setting are techniques used to solidify or firm up ingredients or dishes. It involves cooling them in the refrigerator or freezer to achieve the desired texture and consistency. Chilling is commonly used for setting desserts like puddings, custards, or cheesecakes. It allows the ingredients to firm up and become more stable. By chilling and setting, you can create delicious plant-based desserts that hold their shape and provide a satisfying texture.

Baking and Proofing:
Baking and proofing are techniques primarily used for bread-making. Baking refers to the process of cooking dough or batter in the oven, resulting in bread, rolls, or pastries. Proofing, on the other hand, is the process of allowing the dough to rise and ferment before baking. During proofing, the yeast in the dough produces carbon dioxide, causing the dough to expand and develop a light and airy texture. Mastering baking and proofing techniques allows you to create homemade bread and pastries with a delightful crust and soft interior.

Blanching and Shocking:
Blanching and shocking are techniques used to partially cook vegetables and then rapidly cool them to preserve their vibrant color and texture. Blanching involves briefly boiling the vegetables until they are tender but still crisp. Then, the vegetables are immediately plunged into ice water to stop the cooking process. Blanching and shocking are commonly used for preparing vegetables for salads, stir-fries, or as a prepping step before freezing.

Melting and Tempering Chocolate:
Melting and tempering chocolate are techniques used to achieve smooth and glossy chocolate that has a satisfying snap. Melting chocolate involves gently heating it until it reaches a liquid state, usually done using a double boiler or microwave. Tempering chocolate is the process of carefully manipulating the chocolate's temperature to encourage the formation of stable cocoa butter crystals. This technique ensures that the chocolate sets properly and has a glossy appearance.

Proofing and Baking Yeast-based Doughs:
Proofing and baking yeast-based doughs are techniques used in bread and pastry-making. Proofing involves allowing the yeast in the dough to ferment and produce carbon dioxide, which causes the dough to rise. This process enhances the flavor and texture of the final product. After proofing, the dough is baked at the appropriate temperature to develop a golden crust and a soft interior. Mastering the art of proofing and baking yeast-based doughs allows you to create homemade bread, rolls, and pastries with professional-quality results.

In Chapter 4, we have delved into the essential cooking techniques that are the building blocks of plant-based cuisine. These techniques, from sautéing and roasting to steaming and grilling, empower you to create dishes that are not only delicious but also visually appealing. By understanding and practicing these techniques, you can bring out the natural flavors, textures, and colors of plant-based ingredients, elevating your culinary creations to new heights.

With each technique, you have learned how to manipulate heat, control timing, and experiment with flavors to achieve outstanding results. From marinating and deglazing to tempering chocolate and reducing sauces, these techniques offer a range of options to enhance the taste, texture, and presentation of your plant-based dishes.

As we move forward in our culinary journey, remember that these techniques are not only tools but also gateways to your creativity. Feel free to experiment, innovate, and adapt these techniques to your preferences and dietary needs. The world of plant-based cooking is vast, and by mastering these essential techniques, you have laid a strong foundation for exploring new flavors, textures, and culinary possibilities. So, let's savor the joy of cooking with plant-based ingredients and embark on the next chapter, where we will dive deeper into the art of crafting delicious and nourishing plant-based recipes.

Emerald Apron

Chapter 5

Mastering Flavor Profiles: Spices, Herbs, and Sauces

In Chapter 5, we will explore the world of spices, herbs, and sauces and how they can elevate the flavors of your plant-based dishes. By understanding the art of combining and balancing different flavors, you will gain the skills to create diverse and delicious plant-based meals. We will dive into the characteristics of various spices and herbs, learn how to create homemade sauces, and discover the secrets to achieving harmonious flavor profiles that will leave your taste buds tingling with delight.

Section 1: Exploring Spices

Cumin: Cumin is a warm and earthy spice widely used in cuisines around the world. It adds depth and richness to plant-based dishes, particularly those with legumes, roasted vegetables, or grains. Experiment with toasting cumin seeds before grinding to enhance its flavor.

Paprika: Paprika is a vibrant and smoky spice made from ground dried peppers. It adds a touch of sweetness and mild heat to dishes. Use it to season roasted potatoes, soups, stews, or as a garnish on plant-based proteins.

Turmeric: Turmeric is a bright yellow spice known for its earthy and slightly bitter flavor. It adds a distinctive color to dishes and offers numerous health benefits. Use it in curries, rice dishes, smoothies, or golden milk.

Coriander: Coriander seeds have a citrusy and slightly floral flavor, while fresh cilantro leaves offer a bright and herbaceous taste. Ground coriander is commonly used in spice blends, curries, and marinades, while fresh cilantro adds a fresh kick to salsas, salads, or garnishes.

Cinnamon: Cinnamon is a versatile spice with a warm and sweet flavor. It pairs well with both savory and sweet dishes. Use it in curries, desserts, oatmeal, or sprinkle it on roasted vegetables for a touch of warmth.

Cardamom: Cardamom has a unique and aromatic flavor profile, with hints of citrus and floral notes. It's commonly used in desserts, baked goods, and spice blends. Crush the seeds and add them to dishes or use ground cardamom for convenience.

Chili Powder: Chili powder adds heat and complexity to dishes. It's a blend of ground dried chilies, cumin, garlic, and other spices. Use it to add a kick to chili, Mexican-inspired dishes, or spice rubs for grilled plant-based proteins.

Section 2: Harnessing the Power of Herbs

Basil: Basil is a versatile herb with a sweet and slightly peppery flavor. It pairs well with tomatoes, pasta, salads, and Mediterranean-inspired dishes. Use it fresh or dried, and add it towards the end of cooking for maximum flavor.

Rosemary: Rosemary has a distinct pine-like aroma and a robust flavor. It's commonly used in roasted vegetables, marinades, bread, or infused oils. The woody stems can be used as skewers for grilling plant-based kebabs.

Thyme: Thyme has a subtle and earthy flavor that complements a wide range of dishes. It pairs well with roasted vegetables, soups, stews, and Mediterranean-inspired recipes. Use fresh thyme leaves or dried thyme in your cooking.

Parsley: Parsley offers a fresh and slightly peppery flavor. It's a versatile herb used in salads, dressings, sauces, and garnishes. Flat-leaf (Italian) parsley is preferred for its robust flavor, while curly parsley is commonly used as a garnish.

Dill: Dill has a distinctive flavor with hints of anise and citrus. It adds a refreshing taste to salads, dressings, sauces, and pickles. Use it fresh or dried, and sprinkle it on roasted vegetables or plant-based yogurt.

Mint: Mint has a refreshing and cooling flavor, making it perfect for both savory and sweet dishes. It pairs well with salads, drinks, desserts, and Middle Eastern or Asian-inspired recipes. Use it fresh or dried, and experiment with different varieties like spearmint or peppermint.

Section 3: Creating Homemade Sauces

Tomato Sauce: Tomato sauce is a versatile base for many plant-based dishes. It can be used in pasta dishes, pizzas, stews, or as a dipping sauce. Make your own by sautéing onions and garlic, adding crushed tomatoes, herbs, and seasonings, and simmering until flavors meld together.

Pesto: Pesto is a vibrant sauce made from fresh basil leaves, pine nuts, garlic, olive oil, and Parmesan cheese (vegan alternatives are available). It adds a burst of flavor to pasta, sandwiches, roasted vegetables, or as a dip.

Tahini Sauce: Tahini sauce is a creamy and nutty sauce made from ground sesame seeds. It's a staple in Mediterranean and Middle Eastern cuisines and is used in dishes like hummus, falafel, or as a dressing for salads or roasted vegetables.

Chimichurri: Chimichurri is a tangy and herbaceous sauce originating from Argentina. It's made with fresh herbs like parsley and cilantro, garlic, vinegar, and olive oil. Drizzle it over grilled plant-based proteins, roasted vegetables, or use it as a marinade.

Cashew Cream: Cashew cream is a versatile and dairy-free alternative to traditional cream. Soak raw cashews, blend them with water, and add flavors like lemon juice, nutritional yeast, or spices to create a creamy and luscious sauce. Use it in soups, pasta dishes, or as a base for creamy dressings.

Section 4: Balancing Flavors

Sweetness: Sweetness adds a pleasant and satisfying taste to dishes. Natural sweeteners like maple syrup, agave nectar, or dates can be used to balance the flavors of savory dishes, dressings, or marinades. Experiment with the level of sweetness to achieve the desired balance.

Sourness: Sourness provides a tangy and bright flavor to dishes. Ingredients like citrus juices, vinegars (such as apple cider, balsamic, or rice vinegar), or fermented foods like lemon, lime, or sauerkraut can add a refreshing and zesty touch to your plant-based recipes.

Saltiness: Saltiness enhances and deepens the flavors of ingredients. Opt for sea salt, kosher salt, or tamari (gluten-free soy sauce) to season your dishes. Use it judiciously to avoid overpowering the other flavors.

Umami: Umami is often referred to as the fifth taste and adds depth, richness, and texture to dishes. Ingredients like nutritional yeast, miso paste, soy sauce, tamari, mushrooms, or fermented products like tempeh can contribute to the umami flavor profile of your plant-based creations.

Heat: Heat from spicy ingredients like chili peppers, cayenne pepper, or hot sauces can add a fiery kick to your dishes. Use them sparingly or adjust the heat level to your preference to avoid overwhelming the other flavors.

Section 5: Building Flavor Profiles

Layering Flavors: Building complex flavor profiles involves layering different tastes and aromas. Start with a flavor base of aromatics like onions, garlic, and ginger, then add spices, herbs, and sauces to enhance and complement the base flavors. Experiment with the sequence and intensity of layering to create depth and balance.

Contrast: Incorporating contrasting flavors in a dish can create a harmonious balance. Combining sweet and tangy, spicy and creamy, or earthy and fresh elements can create a delightful interplay of flavors that keep your taste buds engaged.

Regional Cuisines: Explore different regional cuisines to discover unique flavor combinations. From the aromatic spices of Indian cuisine to the herbal infusions of Mediterranean dishes, each cuisine has its own flavor profiles that can inspire your plant-based cooking.

Balancing Intensity: Achieving balance in flavor profiles involves adjusting the intensity of individual flavors. Taste your dishes as you cook and make adjustments as needed. If a dish is too spicy, add sweetness or acidity to balance it out. If it lacks depth, consider adding umami-rich ingredients or adjusting the seasoning.

Section 6: Enhancing Flavor with Texture

Crunchy: Adding a crunchy element to your plant-based dishes can provide a delightful contrast in texture. Consider incorporating ingredients like toasted nuts, seeds, or breadcrumbs to create a satisfying crunch. Sprinkle them over salads, stir-fries, or roasted vegetables for an added textural dimension.

Creamy: Creaminess can add a luxurious and velvety mouthfeel to your dishes. Ingredients like avocado, coconut milk, cashew cream, or plant-based dairy alternatives can be used to create creamy sauces, dressings, or desserts. Experiment with different textures and consistencies to achieve the desired creaminess in your plant-based creations.

Chewy: Introducing chewiness to your dishes can add a satisfying and substantial element. Ingredients like cooked grains, textured vegetable protein (TVP), seitan, or mushrooms can provide a chewy texture in plant-based meals. Consider incorporating them into stir-fries, grain bowls, or plant-based protein dishes for added depth and texture.

Crispy: Crispy textures can elevate the enjoyment of your plant-based dishes. Achieve crispiness by baking, air-frying, or shallow-frying ingredients like tofu, tempeh, or vegetables. The contrast between a crispy exterior and a tender interior can create an exciting sensory experience.

Section 7: Balancing Colors and Presentation

Color Variety: Incorporating a variety of vibrant colors in your dishes not only enhances visual appeal but also indicates a diverse range of nutrients. Consider using a colorful assortment of vegetables, fruits, herbs, and edible flowers to create visually stunning plant-based meals.

Garnishes: Thoughtfully chosen garnishes can add a final touch of visual appeal to your dishes. Sprinkle fresh herbs, toasted seeds, microgreens, or citrus zest over your creations to enhance their appearance. Edible flowers can also lend a beautiful and delicate touch to your plant-based plates.

Plate Composition: Pay attention to the arrangement of your dishes on the plate. Consider the balance of colors, textures, and shapes. Aim for a visually pleasing composition that guides the eye and creates a sense of harmony.

Sauces and Drizzles: Decoratively drizzling or spooning sauces or dressings onto your plates can add artistic flair. Use squeeze bottles or piping bags to create intricate patterns or designs. Sauces can enhance flavors while also adding visual interest to your plant-based dishes.

Section 8: Pairing Flavors and Ingredients

Complementary Pairings: Certain flavors and ingredients naturally complement each other, creating harmonious combinations. For example, pairing the sweetness of roasted carrots with the earthy bitterness of kale or the tanginess of balsamic vinegar can create a well-balanced dish. Consider experimenting with complementary pairings to create complex and enticing flavor profiles in your plant-based meals.

Contrasting Pairings: Contrasting flavors can create exciting and unexpected combinations that awaken the palate. Think about combining the heat of spicy jalapenos with the coolness of creamy avocado or the sweetness of mango with the tang of lime. By juxtaposing different tastes, you can create a dynamic and memorable dining experience.

Regional Flavor Profiles: Explore the culinary traditions of different regions to discover unique flavor pairings. Each cuisine has its own traditional combinations that have stood the test of time. From the sweet and savory flavors of Chinese cuisine to the aromatic and spicy profiles of Indian dishes, these regional flavor pairings can inspire new and exciting creations in your plant-based cooking.

Section 9: Balancing Flavors in Plant-Based Dishes

Taste as You Cook: As you prepare your plant-based dishes, remember to taste and adjust flavors along the way. Take note of the balance between sweetness, sourness, saltiness, umami, and heat. If a dish tastes too sweet, add a touch of acidity or salt to balance it out. If it lacks depth, consider adding umami-rich ingredients or adjusting the seasoning.

Experiment with Spices and Herbs: Spices and herbs play a crucial role in creating flavor profiles. Experiment with different combinations and proportions to achieve the desired taste. Keep in mind that some spices and herbs are more potent than others, so use them sparingly at first and build up as needed.

Consider Textures: Balancing flavors goes beyond taste alone. Texture also plays a role in the overall experience of a dish. Consider the contrast of crunchy and creamy elements, as well as the balance of chewy and tender textures. Combining different textures can add interest and dimension to your plant-based dishes.

Personalize to Taste: Everyone has unique taste preferences, so don't be afraid to personalize recipes to suit your palate. If you prefer more heat, add an extra kick of spice. If you enjoy tanginess, incorporate additional acidic elements. By tailoring flavors to your liking, you can truly make a dish your own.

Section 10: Incorporating Global Flavors

Mexican Flavors: Mexican cuisine is known for its bold and vibrant flavors. Cumin, chili powder, oregano, and cilantro are commonly used spices and herbs that add depth and complexity to dishes. Explore the flavors of salsa, guacamole, and mole to bring a taste of Mexico to your plant-based meals.

Mediterranean Flavors: Mediterranean cuisine offers a diverse range of flavors with ingredients like garlic, lemon, olive oil, oregano, and basil. These flavors can be found in dishes like tabbouleh, falafel, and hummus. Incorporating Mediterranean-inspired flavors can add a fresh and aromatic touch to your plant-based recipes.

Asian Flavors: Asian cuisines, such as Thai, Chinese, Japanese, and Indian, are renowned for their intricate flavor profiles. From the umami-rich sauces of soy, miso, and hoisin to the heat of chili peppers and the freshness of ginger and lemongrass, these flavors can transform your plant-based dishes into culinary masterpieces.

Middle Eastern Flavors: Middle Eastern cuisine showcases an array of spices and herbs like cumin, coriander, turmeric, and sumac. These flavors are found in dishes like falafel, shawarma, and mujadara. Incorporate the warmth and depth of Middle Eastern spices to create enticing and aromatic plant-based meals.

Section 11: Exploring Sauces and Dressings

Vinaigrettes: Vinaigrettes are versatile dressings made from a combination of vinegar or citrus juice, oil, and seasonings. Customize your vinaigrettes with different vinegars, such as balsamic, apple cider, or rice vinegar, and experiment with herbs, mustard, or sweeteners to create a variety of flavor profiles.

Creamy Dressings: Creamy dressings add richness and texture to salads, grain bowls, and sandwiches. Utilize plant-based ingredients like cashews, tahini, silken tofu, or avocado as a base, and add flavors like lemon juice, garlic, herbs, or nutritional yeast to create creamy and flavorful dressings.

Global Sauces: Explore the world of global sauces to enhance your plant-based dishes. From the tangy and spicy sriracha sauce of Southeast Asia to the rich and velvety coconut curry sauce of Indian cuisine, these sauces can elevate the flavors of stir-fries, noodle dishes, and curries.

Nut-Based Sauces: Nut-based sauces provide creaminess and depth of flavor. Experiment with cashew cream, almond butter, or peanut sauce to add richness and complexity to your plant-based recipes. Combine them with spices, herbs, and aromatics for a delectable sauce experience.

Section 12: Meal Planning for Balanced Nutrition

Assessing Macronutrient Needs: When planning plant-based meals, it's essential to ensure you're getting an adequate balance of macronutrients—carbohydrates, proteins, and fats. Incorporate whole grains, legumes, nuts, seeds, and plant-based proteins like tofu, tempeh, or seitan to meet your protein needs. Include a variety of fruits, vegetables, and healthy fats like avocados, olive oil, or nuts to provide carbohydrates and fats.

Portion Control: Pay attention to portion sizes to ensure you're consuming balanced meals. Aim for a plate that is half-filled with vegetables or salads, one-quarter with whole grains or starchy vegetables, and one-quarter with plant-based proteins. Adjust portion sizes based on individual needs and activity levels.

Variety and Color: Include a wide array of fruits, vegetables, whole grains, legumes, and plant-based proteins in your meal plans. This not only provides a range of nutrients but also adds visual appeal and diversity of flavors to your meals. Experiment with different colors, textures, and cooking methods to keep your meals exciting and nutritious.

Nutrient-Dense Foods: Prioritize nutrient-dense foods in your meal plans. These are foods that offer a high amount of vitamins, minerals, and antioxidants per calorie. Leafy greens, cruciferous vegetables, berries, nuts, and seeds are excellent examples. By including these foods, you can ensure you're meeting your nutritional needs while enjoying flavorful and satisfying plant-based meals.

Section 13: Preparing Ahead for Success

Batch Cooking: Allocate time to batch cook ingredients or meals in advance. Cook larger portions of grains, beans, or roasted vegetables that can be stored and used throughout the week. This saves time and ensures you have readily available components to assemble quick and nutritious meals.

Meal Prep Containers: Invest in meal prep containers to portion and store your pre-prepared ingredients or meals. This not only keeps your meals organized but also makes it easy to grab and go, especially for busy days or when you're on the move. Separate containers for grains, proteins, and vegetables allow for easy customization and flexibility.

Freezing: Take advantage of freezing as a preservation method. Cooked grains, beans, soups, and sauces can be portioned and frozen for later use. This allows you to have a variety of options readily available and minimizes food waste.

Planning Tools: Utilize meal planning tools and resources to streamline the process. Online meal planners, smartphone apps, or printable templates can help you organize your meals, create shopping lists, and stay on track with your plant-based eating goals.

Throughout this chapter, we have learned about the importance of layering flavors, the interplay of complementary and contrasting pairings, and the influence of regional cuisines in shaping flavor profiles. We have delved into the world of spices and herbs, exploring their unique characteristics and how they can be harnessed to create extraordinary taste experiences. Additionally, we have embraced the creativity of sauces, learning how to craft homemade dressings and condiments that bring vibrancy to our plant-based dishes.

By mastering the art of flavor profiles, we have expanded our culinary repertoire and gained the confidence to experiment with new ingredients, spices, and herbs. We have discovered the joy of balancing sweetness, sourness, saltiness, umami, and heat in our plant-based creations, creating harmonious and exciting taste sensations. With each exploration, we have broadened our understanding of flavors, deepened our appreciation for diverse cuisines, and embarked on a journey of culinary discovery.

Samin Lisa

Chapter 6

From Farm to Table: Choosing and Preparing Fresh Produce

Welcome to Chapter 6 of "The Green Apron: Plant-Based Made Easy." In this chapter, we will explore the journey of fresh produce from farm to fork. Choosing and preparing fresh fruits and vegetables is a vital aspect of plant-based cooking, as they form the foundation of nutritious and flavorful meals. By understanding how to select the best produce, properly store it, and prepare it for cooking, you can maximize the taste, quality, and nutritional value of your plant-based dishes.

From vibrant and crunchy greens to juicy and ripe fruits, the world of fresh produce offers an abundance of colors, textures, and flavors. We will delve into the importance of selecting seasonal and locally sourced produce, as well as understanding the different varieties and their unique attributes. By making informed choices, you can support local farmers, reduce your carbon footprint, and experience the freshest and most delicious produce available.

But it doesn't stop at the grocery store or farmer's market. Proper storage and preparation techniques are essential to maintain the freshness and integrity of your fruits and vegetables. We will explore best practices for storing different types of produce, including refrigeration, root cellaring, and other preservation methods. Additionally, we will delve into various preparation techniques, such as washing, peeling, and cutting, to ensure optimal flavor and safety.

By brushing up on your skills in choosing and preparing fresh produce, you will not only enhance the taste and nutritional value of your plant-based meals but also cultivate a deeper connection to the ingredients that nourish your body and delight your senses. So, let's embark on this journey from farm to table and unlock the secrets of selecting and preparing the freshest and most vibrant produce for our plant-based creations.

Section 1: Selecting Fresh Produce

Understanding Seasonality: Discover the benefits of choosing produce that is in season. Seasonal fruits and vegetables are not only at their peak flavor and quality, but they are also more readily available and often more affordable. We will explore the seasonal cycles of various produce and learn how to identify when they are at their best.

Locally Sourced Produce: Learn the advantages of supporting local farmers and purchasing locally sourced produce. By doing so, you can reduce the carbon footprint associated with long-distance transportation and support sustainable farming practices in your community. We will discuss ways to connect with local farmers and explore farmer's markets and community-supported agriculture (CSA) programs.

Assessing Quality: Develop an eye for assessing the quality of fresh produce. We will examine the visual cues that indicate freshness, such as vibrant colors, firmness, and absence of bruises or blemishes. Additionally, we will explore the aroma, weight, and other sensory indicators that can help you choose the best produce.

Section 2: Proper Storage and Preservation

Refrigeration Guidelines: Understand the proper storage techniques for different types of produce in the refrigerator. We will discuss the importance of maintaining temperature and humidity levels, storing produce separately to prevent cross-contamination, and utilizing crisper drawers effectively.

Root Cellaring: Discover the age-old method of root cellaring, a traditional way of storing root vegetables, squashes, and other hardy produce. We will explore the basics of root cellaring, including suitable storage conditions, ideal crops for root cellars, and tips for creating a DIY root cellar at home.

Preserving Techniques: Learn various preservation techniques to extend the shelf life of fresh produce. We will cover methods such as canning, pickling, freezing, and dehydrating, providing you with options to enjoy your favorite fruits and vegetables beyond their peak season. Understand the steps involved in each preservation method and gain confidence in preserving the flavors of the harvest.

Section 3: Preparing Fresh Produce

Washing and Cleaning: Master the art of washing and cleaning fresh produce to remove dirt, pesticides, and potential contaminants. We will discuss proper techniques, such as using water, vinegar solutions, or vegetable washes, and explore the importance of thorough rinsing and drying.

Peeling and Cutting: Discover the best practices for peeling and cutting various types of fruits and vegetables. From removing skins to achieving uniform slices or dices, we will cover essential techniques that ensure efficiency and safety in the kitchen. We will also provide tips for preventing browning or oxidation of produce during preparation.

Maximizing Flavor and Nutrition: Explore ways to maximize the flavor and nutritional value of fresh produce. From blanching vegetables to retain their vibrant color and nutrients, to using vegetable scraps for stocks and broths, we will uncover techniques that enhance the taste and health benefits of your plant-based dishes.

Section 4: Reducing Food Waste

Mindful Consumption: Adopt a mindful approach to consuming fresh produce by planning meals, utilizing leftovers, and minimizing waste. We will discuss strategies for meal planning, proper portion sizes, and creative ways to repurpose excess produce to reduce food waste and make the most of your ingredients.

Composting: Learn the basics of composting and how to turn your food scraps and plant-based waste into nutrient-rich compost for your garden. We will cover composting methods, necessary ingredients, and tips for successful composting.

Section 5: Exploring Plant-Based Protein Sources

Legumes: Discover the nutritional powerhouse of legumes, including beans, lentils, and chickpeas. We will explore the variety of legume options, their cooking methods, and how to incorporate them into your plant-based meals. Learn how to prepare delicious dishes like bean soups, lentil stews, and chickpea curries that are not only rich in protein but also packed with fiber and essential nutrients.

Tofu: Dive into the world of tofu, a versatile and protein-rich ingredient derived from soybeans. We will explore different types of tofu, such as silken, firm, and extra-firm, and discuss various cooking methods like baking, grilling, or stir-frying. Discover how tofu can be marinated, seasoned, or incorporated into dishes as a plant-based protein alternative.

Tempeh: Learn about tempeh, a fermented soybean product that offers a unique texture and flavor. We will discuss the health benefits of tempeh, different ways to cook and prepare it, and how to incorporate it into a wide range of recipes. From marinating and grilling to crumbling and sautéing, tempeh adds depth and protein to your plant-based meals.

Seitan: Delve into the world of seitan, a protein-rich ingredient made from wheat gluten. We will explore its versatility in creating meat-like textures and flavors in plant-based dishes. Learn how to make homemade seitan or incorporate store-bought seitan into your recipes. Discover the possibilities of creating seitan-based stir-fries, sandwiches, or even plant-based "meat" substitutes.

Section 6: Balancing Plant-Based Proteins in Meals

Complementary Protein Pairings: Understand the concept of complementary protein pairings to ensure you're obtaining all essential amino acids in your plant-based meals. We will discuss how combining different protein sources, such as legumes and grains, creates a complete protein profile. Explore delicious combinations like beans and rice, lentils and quinoa, or tofu and whole-grain noodles to achieve balanced nutrition.

Plant-Based Protein Powders: Discover the options and considerations when using plant-based protein powders as a supplement or addition to your meals. We will discuss various types of protein powders, including pea, hemp, or brown rice protein, and how to incorporate them into smoothies, baked goods, or energy bars for an extra protein boost.

Snacks and Small Bites: Explore plant-based protein-rich snacks and small bites that can be enjoyed throughout the day. From roasted chickpeas and protein-packed energy balls to edamame and nut butter-dipped fruits, we will provide ideas for convenient and satisfying snacks that keep you fueled and satiated between meals.

Section 7: The Power of Whole Grains

Whole Grain Nutrition: Explore the nutritional benefits of incorporating whole grains into your plant-based diet. Learn about the fiber, vitamins, minerals, and antioxidants present in whole grains and how they contribute to overall health.

Cooking Methods for Whole Grains: Master the various cooking methods for whole grains to achieve optimal taste and texture. Whether it's simmering, steaming, baking, or using a rice cooker or Instant Pot, we will cover techniques to cook different types of whole grains. Understand the water-to-grain ratios, cooking times, and tips for achieving perfectly cooked grains.

Whole Grain Recipe Ideas: Get inspired by a variety of whole grain recipe ideas that showcase the versatility and deliciousness of these nutrient-rich grains. From grain bowls and pilafs to salads and breakfast porridges, we will explore creative and flavorful ways to incorporate whole grains into your meals. Discover the wonderful combinations of flavors and textures that can be achieved with whole grains as the star ingredient.

Section 8: Creative Whole Grain Substitutions

Whole Grain Flour: Experiment with whole grain flours as a substitute for refined flours in your baking endeavors. Discover the unique flavors and textures that whole grain flours bring to bread, pancakes, muffins, and other baked goods. Learn about the different types of whole grain flours, such as whole wheat, spelt, buckwheat, or oat flour, and how to incorporate them into your favorite recipes.

Whole Grain Pasta and Noodles: Explore the world of whole grain pasta and noodles as a healthier alternative to refined versions. From whole wheat spaghetti and brown rice noodles to quinoa pasta and soba noodles, we will discuss the cooking techniques and delicious sauce pairings that bring out the best in these whole grain options.

Whole Grain Snacks and Sides: Discover inventive ways to include whole grains in snacks and side dishes. From crispy whole grain crackers and homemade granola bars to flavorful whole grain salads and pilafs, we will provide recipes and ideas that elevate whole grains beyond their traditional roles.

Section 9: Maximizing Flavor and Texture with Whole Grains

Flavorful Whole Grain Seasonings: Explore the use of seasonings, spices, and herbs to enhance the flavor of whole grains. From adding aromatic herbs like basil or cilantro to incorporating spices like cumin, turmeric, or paprika, we will discuss how these additions can transform simple grains into delicious and satisfying dishes.

Texture Play: Experiment with the texture of whole grains by combining different cooking methods and ingredients. From fluffy and light quinoa to chewy and nutty farro, we will explore the range of textures that can be achieved with whole grains. Discover how to incorporate ingredients like nuts, seeds, dried fruits, or roasted vegetables to add crunch, creaminess, or a burst of flavor to your whole grain creations.

Section 10: The World of Fruits

Nutritional Benefits: Explore the nutritional benefits of incorporating a variety of fruits into your plant-based diet. From vitamins and minerals to fiber and antioxidants, fruits offer a wide range of health-promoting properties. Learn about the specific benefits of different fruits and how they contribute to overall well-being.

Seasonal and Local Options: Embrace the beauty of seasonal and locally sourced fruits. Discover the advantages of choosing fruits that are in season, including superior flavor, higher nutrient content, and support for local farmers. We will discuss the importance of farmers' markets, community-supported agriculture (CSA), and fruit-picking experiences to connect with local produce.

Popular Fruits and Their Uses: Explore popular fruits and their culinary uses. From versatile options like apples, bananas, and berries to exotic choices like mangoes, papayas, and dragon fruit, we will delve into the unique flavors, textures, and ways to incorporate these fruits into your plant-based meals. Discover ideas for fresh fruit salads, smoothies, desserts, and more.

Section 11: The Vibrancy of Vegetables

Nutritional Powerhouses: Uncover the nutritional powerhouses that vegetables offer. From leafy greens and cruciferous vegetables to root vegetables and vibrant peppers, vegetables are packed with vitamins, minerals, and phytonutrients. We will explore the specific health benefits of different vegetable groups and how to maximize their nutritional value.

Understanding Cooking Methods: Master the different cooking methods for vegetables to achieve optimal taste, texture, and nutrient retention. Whether it's sautéing, roasting, steaming, grilling, or blanching, we will cover techniques that bring out the natural flavors and textures of various vegetables. Discover which cooking methods work best for specific vegetables and how to retain their vibrant colors.

Creative Vegetable Preparations: Embrace the creativity of vegetable preparations in your plant-based cooking. From spiralizing zucchini into "noodles" to using cauliflower rice as a low-carb alternative, we will explore innovative ways to incorporate vegetables into your favorite dishes. Learn how to make vegetable-based sauces, dips, and even desserts for a fun and nutritious twist.

Section 12: Flavorful Herb and Spice Pairings

Enhancing Flavor with Herbs: Discover the world of herbs and how they can elevate the flavors of fruits and vegetables. From aromatic herbs like basil, mint, and cilantro to woody herbs like rosemary, thyme, and sage, we will explore the unique qualities of different herbs and their compatibility with various fruits and vegetables.

Spice Up Your Dishes: Delve into the realm of spices and their transformative impact on plant-based cooking. From warming spices like cinnamon, nutmeg, and cloves to bold spices like cumin, paprika, and turmeric, we will discuss the distinct flavors and health benefits that spices bring to fruits and vegetables. Learn how to use spices to create depth, complexity, and cultural authenticity in your dishes.

Balancing Flavors: Understand the art of balancing flavors when combining fruits, vegetables, herbs, and spices. Discover how the sweet, sour, salty, bitter, and umami tastes can be harmonized to create well-rounded and delicious dishes. Gain insight into proper seasoning techniques and the impact of acidity, salt, and other flavor elements on fruits and vegetables.

Section 13: Embracing Healthy Plant-Based Fats

The Role of Healthy Fats: Understand the importance of incorporating healthy fats into a plant-based diet. Learn about the different types of fats, including monounsaturated fats, polyunsaturated fats, and omega-3 fatty acids, and their role in supporting brain health, hormone production, and overall well-being.

Avocado: Discover the creamy and nutritious goodness of avocados. From guacamole and avocado toast to smoothies and salad dressings, explore the versatility of avocados and their ability to add richness and healthy fats to a wide range of plant-based dishes.

Nuts and Seeds: Delve into the world of nuts and seeds, packed with essential fatty acids, vitamins, minerals, and antioxidants. Explore the variety of options, from almonds and walnuts to chia seeds and flaxseeds, and learn how to incorporate them into your meals and snacks. Discover how to make nut butters, seed crackers, and homemade granolas for a delightful dose of healthy fats.

Plant-Based Oils: Understand the role of plant-based oils in cooking and flavor enhancement. From olive oil and coconut oil to sesame oil and avocado oil, we will explore the characteristics of different oils and their culinary uses. Learn about proper storage, smoke points, and how to choose the right oil for various cooking methods.

Section 14: Creative Ways to Use Plant-Based Fats

Dressings and Sauces: Discover how plant-based fats can be used to create delicious dressings and sauces. From tahini-based dressings to cashew cream sauces, we will explore the versatility of plant-based fats in enhancing the flavors of salads, roasted vegetables, grain bowls, and more.

Baking with Plant-Based Fats: Learn how to substitute plant-based fats in your baking endeavors. Explore options like applesauce, mashed bananas, nut butters, or coconut oil as alternatives to butter and eggs. Discover how these substitutions can create moist and flavorful plant-based baked goods.

Plant-Based Spreads and Dips: Get creative with plant-based spreads and dips that incorporate healthy fats. From hummus and guacamole to almond butter and cashew cheese, we will explore homemade recipes and ideas for nutritious and delicious spreads that can be enjoyed with crackers, raw veggies, or sandwiches.

Section 15: Balancing Healthy Fats in a Plant-Based Diet

Portion Control and Moderation: Understand the importance of portion control and moderation when it comes to consuming healthy fats. While they offer numerous health benefits, it's essential to strike a balance and not exceed recommended intake levels. Learn how to incorporate healthy fats into your meals without overdoing it.

Omega-3 Fatty Acids: Explore the benefits of omega-3 fatty acids and how to ensure an adequate intake on a plant-based diet. Discover plant-based sources of omega-3s, such as flaxseeds, chia seeds, hemp seeds, and walnuts, and learn how to incorporate them into your meals for optimal health.

Chapter 6 has taken us on a journey from the farm to our table, exploring the importance of choosing and preparing fresh produce in our plant-based meals. We have learned the significance of selecting seasonal and locally sourced produce, understanding quality indicators, and adopting proper storage and preparation techniques. By embracing the journey of fresh produce, we can unlock the full potential of our ingredients and create nourishing, flavorful, and vibrant plant-based dishes.

Throughout this chapter, we have showcased the diversity and abundance of fruits and vegetables, recognizing their nutritional benefits, culinary versatility, and the creative possibilities they offer. We have discovered the power of seasonality, supporting local farmers, and connecting with the natural cycles of produce. By choosing fruits and vegetables that are in season, we not only access their peak flavors and nutrients but also contribute to sustainable food systems.

Additionally, we have explored the art of proper storage and preservation, understanding the nuances of refrigeration, root cellaring, and other methods to extend the shelf life of our produce. By utilizing these techniques, we can reduce waste and maximize the freshness and nutritional value of our fruits and vegetables.

Moreover, we have delved into the essential skills of washing, peeling, and cutting fresh produce, ensuring food safety, and optimizing flavor. By mastering these techniques, we can enhance the quality and appeal of our plant-based dishes, allowing the natural beauty and taste of the produce to shine through.

As we conclude Chapter 6, let us reflect on the beauty and nourishment that fresh produce brings to our plates. By embracing the journey from farm to table, we honor the hard work of farmers, the richness of the land, and the vibrant colors and flavors that nature offers us. Let us continue to celebrate and appreciate the remarkable world of fruits and vegetables as we embark on our plant-based culinary adventures.

Samin Lisa

Chapter 7

Powerhouse Proteins: Incorporating Plant-Based Protein Sources

Welcome to Chapter 7 of "The Green Apron: Plant-Based Made Easy." In this chapter, we will delve into the realm of powerhouse proteins and explore the diverse and delicious plant-based sources that provide us with the essential building blocks of life. As we embark on our plant-based journey, it is essential to understand the importance of protein and how to incorporate it into our meals in a sustainable and nourishing way.

Protein is an essential macronutrient that plays a vital role in our overall health and well-being. It is responsible for building and repairing tissues, supporting immune function, and aiding in the production of enzymes and hormones. While animal products have long been associated with protein, plant-based sources offer a wealth of protein-rich options that are not only nutritious but also environmentally friendly and compassionate.

In this chapter, we will explore a variety of plant-based protein sources, from legumes and tofu to tempeh and seitan. We will dive into the nutritional benefits, culinary versatility, and cooking techniques associated with each source. By understanding the unique qualities of different plant-based proteins, we can create well-balanced and satisfying meals that meet our nutritional needs.

As we embrace plant-based proteins, we also celebrate the sustainability and ethical considerations that come with this dietary choice. By shifting our focus to plant-based sources, we reduce the environmental impact associated with animal agriculture, conserve precious resources, and contribute to a more compassionate and equitable food system.

Section 1: Legumes: Nature's Protein Powerhouses

Legumes: Explore the incredible world of legumes, including beans, lentils, chickpeas, and peas. These humble yet mighty plant-based proteins are not only rich in protein but also packed with fiber, vitamins, minerals, and antioxidants. We will discuss the nutritional benefits, various types of legumes, and ways to incorporate them into our meals. From hearty bean soups and comforting lentil stews to flavorful chickpea curries and satisfying pea-based dishes, legumes offer endless possibilities in the plant-based kitchen.

Tofu: Discover the versatility of tofu, a staple in many plant-based diets. Made from soybeans, tofu is a complete protein source that can be prepared in various ways to create a range of textures and flavors. We will explore the different types of tofu, such as silken, firm, and extra-firm, and discuss techniques for marinating, grilling, baking, or stir-frying tofu. Whether used as a meat substitute or as a key ingredient in Asian-inspired dishes, tofu provides a satisfying protein boost to our meals.

Section 2: Fermented Delights: Tempeh and Seitan

Tempeh: Journey into the world of tempeh, a fermented soybean product originating from Indonesia that offers a unique taste and texture. Tempeh is a protein-rich food that also contains probiotics, making it beneficial for gut health. We will explore the process of fermenting soybeans into tempeh, discuss the nutritional benefits, and learn how to cook and incorporate this versatile ingredient into our plant-based recipes. From tempeh bacon and stir-fries to burgers and hearty salads, tempeh adds a hearty and nutritious element to our meals.

Seitan: Delve into the world of seitan, a protein-packed meat substitute made from wheat gluten. Seitan is known for its meaty texture and ability to absorb flavors. We will explore the process of creating seitan from wheat gluten, discuss its nutritional profile, and discover different cooking methods and recipe ideas. From seitan-based stir-fries and sandwiches to plant-based "meat" substitutes, seitan offers a versatile and protein-rich addition to our plant-based culinary repertoire.

Section 3: Balancing Protein Intake and Complementary Sources

Complete vs. Incomplete Proteins: Understand the concept of complete and incomplete proteins and the importance of balancing protein intake on a plant-based diet. We will explore how to combine different plant-based protein sources to ensure we obtain all essential amino acids. Discover complementary protein pairings such as legumes and grains, which create a complete protein profile and provide the necessary building blocks for our bodies.

Nuts and Seeds: While they may not be complete protein sources on their own, they offer valuable protein, healthy fats, vitamins, minerals, and antioxidants. We will discuss the nutritional benefits of various nuts and seeds, their culinary uses, and creative ways to incorporate them into our meals. From homemade nut butters and seed-based energy bars to sprinkling them over salads and incorporating them into baked goods, nuts and seeds add a delightful crunch and protein boost to our plant-based dishes.

Plant-Based Protein Powders: We will explore various types of protein powders, including pea, hemp, brown rice, and soy, and discuss their nutritional profiles and potential benefits. Learn how to incorporate protein powders into smoothies, shakes, baked goods, or homemade protein bars for an extra protein boost when needed.

Section 4: Protein-Rich Whole Grains and Pseudo Grains

Quinoa: Explore the protein-rich qualities of quinoa, a versatile and complete plant-based protein source. We will delve into the nutritional benefits of quinoa, different varieties available, and ways to incorporate this ancient grain into our meals. From quinoa salads and pilafs to porridges and veggie burgers, quinoa offers a satisfying and protein-packed base for a variety of dishes.

Amaranth and Buckwheat: Discover the protein powerhouses of amaranth and buckwheat, two lesser known yet highly nutritious pseudo grains. These gluten-free options are rich in protein, fiber, and essential minerals. We will explore their culinary uses, cooking methods, and how to incorporate them into our plant-based recipes. From amaranth porridge and buckwheat pancakes to savory pilafs and creative grain bowls, these pseudo grains provide a delightful and nutritious alternative to traditional grains.

Section 5: Maximizing Protein Intake for Athletes and Active Lifestyles

Plant-Based Protein for Athletes: Understand the protein needs of athletes and those with active lifestyles on a plant-based diet. We will explore the importance of timing protein intake, choosing high-quality sources, and incorporating a variety of plant-based protein sources to meet the demands of physical activity. Discover plant-based protein-rich meals, snacks, and recovery options that support optimal performance and muscle repair.

Protein Pairings for Vegans and Vegetarians: Address the common concern of protein adequacy in vegan and vegetarian diets. We will provide guidance on achieving balanced protein intake through strategic food combinations and meal planning. Learn about creative protein pairings, such as legumes and grains, nuts and seeds, and tofu and whole grains, to ensure a well-rounded and satisfying protein profile.

Section 6: Maximizing Protein Intake for Athletes and Active Lifestyles

Plant-Based Protein for Athletes: Athletes and individuals with active lifestyles have unique protein needs to support muscle growth, repair, and recovery. While plant-based sources can meet these needs, it is essential to understand the timing and quantity of protein intake. We will discuss strategies for incorporating plant-based proteins before and after workouts to optimize muscle protein synthesis. Additionally, we will explore protein-rich plant-based meals, snacks, and shakes that provide the necessary amino acids and nutrients for athletic performance.

Protein Pairings for Vegans and Vegetarians: Vegans and vegetarians can easily meet their protein requirements by strategically combining plant-based protein sources. We will delve into the concept of protein complementation, where different plant-based foods are paired to form a complete protein profile. For example, combining legumes and grains, such as lentils and rice or chickpeas and quinoa, creates a complementary amino acid profile. We will provide practical examples of protein-rich meals and snacks that incorporate these complementary protein sources, ensuring a well-rounded and satisfying protein intake.

Section 7: Exploring Plant-Based Protein Powders

Types of Plant-Based Protein Powders: Protein powders derived from plant sources have gained popularity as a convenient way to supplement protein intake. We will explore different types of plant-based protein powders, such as pea, hemp, rice, and soy. Each type offers unique nutritional profiles and amino acid profiles, catering to individual dietary preferences and requirements. We will discuss the benefits, potential allergens, and taste profiles of each protein powder, allowing you to make informed choices when selecting a plant-based protein powder.

Incorporating Protein Powders into Recipes: Protein powders can be incorporated into a wide range of recipes, adding a protein boost to various meals and snacks. We will provide ideas for incorporating plant-based protein powders into smoothies, energy bars, pancakes, muffins, and homemade protein shakes. With these creative and delicious recipes, you can enjoy the benefits of protein powders while enjoying the flavors and textures of your favorite plant-based treats.

Section 8: Plant-Based Protein for Children and Adolescents

Meeting Protein Needs in Childhood: Protein is crucial for growth and development in children and adolescents. We will discuss how to meet their protein needs on a plant-based diet, ensuring they receive adequate nutrition for healthy growth and development. We will explore plant-based protein sources that are kid-friendly, such as legumes, tofu, and nut butters. Additionally, we will provide guidance on meal planning and creating balanced, protein-rich meals that children will enjoy.

Plant-Based Protein for Teenagers: Teenagers have increased protein needs due to growth spurts, hormone changes and increased physical activity. We will discuss strategies for meeting their protein requirements on a plant-based diet, including protein-rich meals and snacks that are appealing to teenagers. We will explore plant-based protein sources that can be easily incorporated into their meals, such as plant-based burgers, smoothies, sandwiches, and wraps. By providing nutritious and protein-rich options, we can support their overall health and well-being during this critical stage of life.

Section 9: Incorporating Protein-Rich Grains and Seeds

Quinoa: Quinoa is a unique plant-based protein source that is also considered a pseudo-grain. It is a complete protein, meaning it contains all essential amino acids. Quinoa is versatile and can be used as a base for salads, pilafs, and even breakfast porridge. Its nutty flavor and fluffy texture make it a delightful addition to a variety of plant-based dishes.

Chia Seeds: Chia seeds may be small, but they pack a powerful nutritional punch. They are an excellent source of protein, fiber, and omega-3 fatty acids. Chia seeds can be added to smoothies, oatmeal, yogurt, or used as an egg substitute in baking recipes. They absorb liquid and form a gel-like consistency, adding a unique texture and nutritional boost to your meals.

Hemp Seeds: Hemp seeds are rich in protein, healthy fats, and essential fatty acids. They have a mild, nutty flavor and can be sprinkled over salads, blended into smoothies, or used as a topping for roasted vegetables. Hemp seeds are a complete protein source and offer additional nutritional benefits such as fiber and minerals.

Flaxseeds: Flaxseeds are another protein-rich option that also provides omega-3 fatty acids and fiber. Ground flaxseeds can be incorporated into baking recipes, smoothies, or sprinkled over cereals and yogurt for a nutritional boost. Remember to grind flaxseeds before consuming them to ensure optimal absorption of nutrients.

Section 10: Protein-Rich Plant-Based Dairy Alternatives

Soy Products: Soy-based products like tofu, tempeh, and edamame are excellent sources of plant-based protein. Tofu is versatile and can be used in stir-fries, soups, or marinated and grilled for a delicious main course. Tempeh has a firm texture and nutty flavor, making it a great addition to sandwiches, salads, or stir-fries. Edamame, young soybeans, can be enjoyed as a snack, added to salads, or incorporated into Asian-inspired dishes.

Plant-Based Yogurt: Many plant-based yogurts are fortified with protein derived from sources like soy, almond, or pea protein. Look for options with a higher protein content to boost your protein intake. Plant-based yogurt can be enjoyed on its own, topped with fruits and nuts, or used in smoothies, sauces, and baked goods.

Section 11: Protein-Packed Plant-Based Snacks

Nut and Seed Butters: Nut and seed butters, such as almond butter, peanut butter, or sunflower seed butter, are not only delicious but also provide a good amount of protein and healthy fats. They can be spread on toast, used as a dip for fruits and vegetables, or incorporated into energy bars and homemade granola.

Protein Bars and Energy Balls: Look for plant-based protein bars and energy balls that are made with natural ingredients and contain a good balance of protein, carbohydrates, and healthy fats. These convenient snacks can be enjoyed on the go or as a post-workout refuel.

Roasted Chickpeas: Roasted chickpeas are a crunchy and protein-rich snack that can be seasoned with various spices and herbs. They make a great alternative to processed snack foods and can be enjoyed on their own or sprinkled over salads for added texture and flavor.

Section 12: Protein-Rich Smoothies and Beverages

Plant-Based Protein Smoothies: Smoothies are a refreshing and convenient way to incorporate protein into your diet. By blending together a combination of plant-based proteins, fruits, vegetables, and liquids, you can create a satisfying and nutrient-dense beverage. Explore protein-rich ingredients such as silken tofu, plant-based protein powders, Greek-style yogurt alternatives, or nut butters to enhance the protein content of your smoothies. Experiment with different flavor combinations and add-ins like spinach, berries, bananas, or seeds for added nutrients and variety.

Plant-Based Protein Shakes: Protein shakes are a popular option for those seeking a quick and convenient protein boost. Look for plant-based protein powders that align with your dietary preferences and needs. Consider options like pea protein, hemp protein, or a blend of various plant-based protein sources. Mix the protein powder with your choice of liquid, such as almond milk, coconut water, or dairy-free milk alternatives, and enjoy a protein-rich beverage post-workout or as a snack throughout the day.

Section 13: Protein-Rich Salads and Bowls

Protein-Packed Salad Ingredients: Salads can be an excellent vehicle for incorporating protein-rich ingredients into your meals. Choose a variety of vegetables, leafy greens, and add protein sources such as cooked lentils, chickpeas, grilled tofu, or tempeh. Top your salad with a drizzle of tahini dressing or a sprinkle of seeds for added texture and flavor. Consider adding whole grains like quinoa or farro to make your salad even more filling and nutritious.

Plant-Based Protein Bowls: Protein bowls are a satisfying and well-balanced meal option. Start with a base of cooked grains like brown rice, quinoa, or barley. Add a variety of protein sources such as roasted chickpeas, marinated tofu, or seitan. Include a colorful array of roasted or sautéed vegetables for added nutrients and flavor. Finish off your bowl with a flavorful sauce or dressing to tie everything together.

Section 14: Protein-Packed Plant-Based Desserts

Bean-Based Desserts: Believe it or not, beans can be a surprising and nutritious addition to your sweet treats. They can be used to create protein-rich desserts like black bean brownies, chickpea blondies, or kidney bean truffles. By combining beans with ingredients like cocoa powder, nut butter, and natural sweeteners, you can indulge in delicious desserts that also provide a protein boost.

Chia Seed Puddings: Chia seed puddings are a simple and nutritious dessert option that is packed with plant-based protein. Soak chia seeds in your choice of plant-based milk, sweeten with natural sweeteners like maple syrup or dates, and let them set overnight. In the morning, you'll have a creamy and protein-rich pudding that can be topped with fruits, nuts, or granola for added texture and flavor.

Section 15: Protein-Focused Meal Prepping

Protein-Packed Meal Prep Ideas: Meal prepping can help you stay on track with your protein goals throughout the week. Plan and prepare protein-rich meals in advance to ensure you have balanced and nutritious options readily available. Consider batch-cooking ingredients like quinoa, lentils, or roasted tofu that can be used as a base for various meals. Prepare containers of pre-portioned salads, grain bowls, or stir-fries that include a combination of protein sources, vegetables, and whole grains. Having protein-focused meal options ready to go will save you time and make it easier to maintain a plant-based diet.

Protein-Rich Snack Prep: Prepare protein-packed snacks to have on hand when hunger strikes. Portion out servings of roasted chickpeas, trail mix with nuts and seeds, or homemade protein bars into individual containers or resealable bags. Chop vegetables and prepare homemade hummus or bean dip for dipping. By having these protein-rich snacks prepped and ready, you can avoid reaching for less nutritious options when you're in need of a quick bite.

We have learned how to incorporate an array of protein sources into our meals, from legumes and tofu to quinoa and chia seeds. By embracing these protein-rich options, we have expanded our culinary horizons and discovered new and exciting ways to nourish our bodies with plant-based proteins.

Incorporating these protein sources into our meals allows us to create a well-rounded and balanced plant-based diet. By combining different protein-rich ingredients, we can ensure that we are meeting our nutritional needs and fueling our bodies with the building blocks necessary for optimal health and well-being.

Furthermore, embracing plant-based proteins supports our commitment to sustainability and the environment. Plant-based proteins have a significantly lower carbon footprint compared to animal-based proteins. By choosing legumes, tofu, and other plant-based options, we reduce the strain on our planet's resources and contribute to a more ecologically-positive food system.

Emerald Apron

Chapter 8

Grains, Legumes, and Seeds: Nutrient-Rich Staples for Every Meal

In this chapter, we will delve into the world of grains, legumes, and seeds, exploring their nutritional benefits, cooking techniques, and creative ways to incorporate them into our plant-based meals. These nutrient-rich staples form the foundation of many cuisines around the world and provide a wealth of health-promoting properties.

Grains, legumes, and seeds offer a wide range of essential nutrients, including complex carbohydrates, dietary fiber, vitamins, minerals, and plant-based proteins. Incorporating them into our meals not only adds texture, flavor, and variety but also supports our overall well-being. When we utilize our understanding the unique qualities of different grains, legumes, and seeds, we can create delicious and nourishing plant-based dishes that are satisfying and nutrient-dense.

Section 1: Exploring Grains

Grains have been a dietary staple for centuries, providing sustenance and nourishment to civilizations around the globe. They come in various forms, including rice, wheat, oats, barley, quinoa, millet, and more. Each grain offers its own nutritional profile and culinary characteristics, making them versatile ingredients for a wide range of dishes.

Rice: Rice is a staple grain in many cultures and comes in different varieties such as white, brown, black, and wild rice. Brown rice, in particular, is a nutritious whole grain that retains its bran and germ layers, offering fiber, vitamins, and minerals. It can be used as a base for stir-fries, pilafs, or grain bowls.

Wheat: Wheat is a widely consumed grain, especially in the form of flour used for baking bread, pastries, and pasta. Whole wheat products, such as whole wheat bread or whole wheat pasta, retain the nutrient-rich bran and germ, providing fiber, B-vitamins, and minerals. Experiment with different types of wheat-based products, opting for whole grain options whenever possible.

Oats: Oats are a versatile grain that can be enjoyed as oatmeal, used in baking, or added to smoothies. They are an excellent source of soluble fiber, which helps to lower cholesterol levels and promote digestive health. Rolled oats, steel-cut oats, or quick oats can be used depending on the desired texture and cooking time.

Quinoa: Quinoa is a pseudo-grain that is often referred to as a "superfood" due to its exceptional nutritional profile. It is a complete protein, meaning it contains all nine essential amino acids, making it an excellent plant-based protein source. Quinoa is also rich in dietary fiber, vitamins, and minerals. Use it as a base for salads, pilafs, or stuffed peppers for a nutrient-packed meal.

Section 2: Using Beans and Legumes

Legumes, including beans, lentils, chickpeas, and peas, are nutrient-dense powerhouses that offer a wide range of health benefits. They are an excellent source of plant-based protein, fiber, complex carbohydrates, vitamins, minerals, and phytochemicals. Legumes come in various forms, including canned, dried, or sprouted, and can be incorporated into a variety of dishes.

Beans: Beans, such as black beans, kidney beans, pinto beans, or navy beans, are versatile and widely used in many cuisines. They are rich in protein, dietary fiber, iron, and folate. Incorporate beans into soups, stews, chili, salads, or as a filling for burritos and tacos. You can use canned beans for convenience or cook dried beans for a more economical option.

Lentils: Lentils are a quick-cooking legume that comes in various colors, including green, brown, red, and black. They are an excellent source of protein, dietary fiber, and folate. Use lentils in soups, curries, salads, or as a meat substitute in dishes like lentil loaf or lentil burgers. They absorb flavors well and provide a hearty texture to your meals.

Chickpeas: Chickpeas, also known as garbanzo beans, are versatile legumes with a mild nutty flavor. They are a great source of plant-based protein, dietary fiber, and folate. Use chickpeas in hummus, falafel, curries, or roast them for a crunchy snack. You can also mash them to create a vegan-friendly alternative to tuna or chicken salad.

Section 3: Harnessing the Power of Seeds

Seeds are often overlooked but are nutrient powerhouses that can add a nutritional boost to our meals. They are rich in healthy fats, protein, dietary fiber, vitamins, minerals, and antioxidants. Incorporating seeds into our diet can enhance the nutritional profile of our meals and provide a satisfying crunch. The use of seeds in cooking is an easy way to add vital nutrients and texture to your meals. They're also great for snacking on.

Chia Seeds: Chia seeds are a tiny but mighty seed packed with omega-3 fatty acids, protein, dietary fiber, and antioxidants. They can absorb liquid and form a gel-like consistency, making them a great addition to smoothies, puddings, or as an egg substitute in baking. Sprinkle chia seeds over cereals, yogurt, or salads for added texture and nutritional value.

Flaxseeds: Flaxseeds are rich in omega-3 fatty acids, dietary fiber, lignans, and antioxidants. They have a mild, nutty flavor and can be ground and used as an egg substitute in baking or added to smoothies, oatmeal, or yogurt. To enjoy their nutritional benefits, it is best to consume ground flaxseeds as whole flaxseeds may pass through the digestive system undigested.

Sesame Seeds: Sesame seeds are a common ingredient in Asian cuisine and offer a nutty flavor and delicate crunch. They are a good source of protein, healthy fats, dietary fiber, and various minerals like calcium, iron, and zinc. Sprinkle sesame seeds over stir-fries, salads, or use them as a coating for tofu or roasted vegetables.

Pumpkin Seeds: Pumpkin seeds, also known as pepitas, are a great source of protein, healthy fats, dietary fiber, and minerals like magnesium and zinc. Roast pumpkin seeds for a crunchy snack, sprinkle them over salads, or incorporate them into baked goods like bread or muffins for added texture and nutritional benefits.

Section 4: Creative Ways to Incorporate Grains, Legumes, and Seeds

Grain Salads and Bowls: Use cooked grains like quinoa, brown rice, or farro as a base for hearty salads or grain bowls. Add a variety of vegetables, legumes, and seeds for a nutrient-packed meal. Toss with a flavorful dressing or sauce to bring all the ingredients together.

Grain and Legume Soups: Combine grains and legumes in comforting soups to create a satisfying and nutritious meal. For example, lentil soup with barley or black bean and quinoa chili. These soups provide a balanced combination of protein, fiber, and complex carbohydrates.

Seed Toppings and Mixes: Sprinkle seeds over salads, roasted vegetables, or grain dishes to add texture, flavor, and a nutritional boost. You can also create your own seed mixes by combining different seeds like sunflower seeds, pumpkin seeds, and sesame seeds. Use these mixes as a topping for yogurt, smoothie bowls, or as a crunchy addition to baked goods.

Homemade Nut and Seed Butters: Experiment with making your own nut and seed butters using ingredients like almonds, walnuts, sunflower seeds, or pumpkin seeds. These spreads can be enjoyed on toast, added to smoothies, or used as a base for sauces and dressings.

Section 5: Cooking Techniques for Grains, Legumes, and Seeds

Cooking Grains: Different grains require various cooking techniques to achieve the desired texture and flavor. Follow package instructions for cooking times and water ratios. However, here are some general tips:

For fluffy rice, use a 1:2 ratio of rice to water and cook covered over low heat until the water is absorbed.

Whole grains like quinoa and farro can be cooked in a similar manner to rice but may require slightly longer cooking times.

Oats can be cooked on the stovetop or in the microwave with a 1:2 ratio of oats to liquid, whether it's water or plant-based milk. Simmer or microwave until the oats are tender.

Preparing Legumes: Legumes can be cooked from dried or canned forms. Here are some guidelines:

To cook dried legumes, soak them overnight in water, then drain and rinse. Place the legumes in a pot, cover with fresh water, and simmer until tender. The cooking time will vary depending on the type of legume, so refer to specific instructions.

Canned legumes are pre-cooked and can be rinsed and drained before using. They are convenient for quick meals and can be added to salads, soups, stews, or mashed for spreads like hummus.

Toasting Seeds: Toasting seeds enhances their flavor and adds a delightful crunch. To toast seeds, heat a dry skillet over medium heat and add the seeds. Stir them constantly for a few minutes until they become golden brown and fragrant. Watch them carefully to avoid burning.

Sprouting Legumes and Seeds: Sprouting legumes and seeds can increase their nutritional value and make them easier to digest. Soak the legumes or seeds in water for several hours, then drain and rinse them. Place them in a sprouting jar or tray and follow specific instructions for the desired sprouting time. Rinse them daily until they sprout, and enjoy them in salads, wraps, or as a crunchy snack.

Section 6: Creative Meal Ideas with Grains, Legumes, and Seeds

Buddha Bowls: Create nourishing Buddha bowls by combining cooked grains, legumes, and an assortment of vegetables. Top with a flavorful dressing or sauce for a complete and satisfying meal.

Grain-based Salads: Mix cooked grains with fresh vegetables, herbs, and a protein source like beans or lentils. Drizzle with a zesty vinaigrette for a refreshing and nutritious salad.

Legume-based Curries: Prepare delicious curries by combining cooked legumes with aromatic spices, vegetables, and creamy coconut milk. Serve over cooked grains or with flatbread for a comforting and flavorful meal.

Seed Energy Bars: Make your own energy bars using a combination of seeds, nuts, dried fruits, and natural sweeteners. These homemade bars are a great snack option for a quick burst of energy.

Section 7: Maximizing Nutrition with Grains, Legumes, and Seeds

Pairing Grains with Legumes: Combining grains and legumes creates a complete protein source, as the amino acids in each complement each other. For example, rice and beans, whole wheat bread with hummus, or quinoa with lentils. These combinations provide a balanced meal with essential amino acids.

Soaking and Fermenting: Soaking grains, legumes, and seeds before cooking can help improve their digestibility and nutrient absorption. Fermenting grains and legumes through methods like sourdough bread or fermented soy products like tempeh can enhance their nutritional value and promote gut health.

Incorporating Sprouted Varieties: Sprouted grains, legumes, and seeds offer increased nutrient availability and can be used in a variety of dishes. Look for sprouted versions or sprout them at home to reap their benefits.

Section 8: Enhancing Flavor with Grains, Legumes, and Seeds

Toasted Grain and Seed Pilafs: Toasting grains and seeds before cooking adds a nutty flavor and enhances their aroma. Prepare pilafs by sautéing toasted grains and seeds in oil or vegan butter, then adding broth or water to cook them. Customize your pilaf with aromatic herbs and spices for a delightful and flavorful side dish.

Grain and Legume Stews: Create hearty and flavorful stews by combining cooked grains and legumes with vegetables, herbs, and spices. Simmer them together in a flavorful broth until the flavors meld and the ingredients become tender. Adjust the seasonings to suit your taste preferences, and serve the stew with crusty bread for a comforting and nourishing meal.

Seasoned Roasted Grains and Seeds: Roasting grains and seeds can enhance their flavor and add a delightful crunch to your dishes. Toss cooked grains and seeds with your favorite seasonings, such as smoked paprika, garlic powder, or dried herbs. Spread them on a baking sheet and roast in the oven until they turn golden and crispy. These seasoned roasted grains and seeds can be used as a topping for salads, soups, or grain bowls, or enjoyed as a standalone snack.

Section 9: Gluten-Free Options and Alternatives

Gluten-Free Grains: For those following a gluten-free diet, there are plenty of grain options to choose from. Incorporate gluten-free grains like quinoa, amaranth, buckwheat, millet, and rice into your meals. Experiment with different combinations and cooking methods to discover new flavors and textures.

Legume and Seed Flours: If you're looking for gluten-free alternatives to traditional wheat flour, consider using legume and seed flours. Chickpea flour, lentil flour, and almond flour are versatile options that can be used in baking, breading, or as a thickening agent. They offer a nutritional boost and add unique flavors to your dishes.

Section 10: Fermented and Cultured Options

Fermented Grains and Legumes: Fermentation is a process that enhances the flavor, digestibility, and nutritional profile of grains and legumes. Fermented options like tempeh, miso, and sourdough bread provide probiotics and can be used to add depth and tang to your meals. Incorporate these fermented foods into stir-fries, sandwiches, or dressings for a unique and delicious twist.

Sprouted Grains and Legumes: Sprouting grains and legumes increases their nutrient availability and reduces anti-nutrients. Sprouted grains and legumes can be used in a variety of dishes, including salads, wraps, or added to stir-fries. They provide a fresh and crunchy texture while offering enhanced nutritional benefits.

Section 11: Grains, Legumes, and Seeds for Desserts

Whole Grain Desserts: Explore the world of whole grain desserts by incorporating grains like oats, quinoa, or buckwheat into baked goods. Try recipes for whole grain cookies, muffins, or cakes that offer a wholesome twist on traditional sweets. These desserts provide the added benefits of fiber and nutrients.

Legume and Seed-Based Treats: Legumes and seeds can be used to create delicious and nutrient-rich desserts. Experiment with chickpea flour to make gluten-free brownies, use almond flour to prepare a nutty tart crust, or incorporate ground flaxseeds into vegan baking recipes. These alternatives not only provide unique flavors but also offer a nutritional boost to your sweet treats.

Section 12: Incorporating Grains, Legumes, and Seeds into Breakfast

Breakfast Grain Bowls: Start your day with a nourishing grain bowl by combining cooked grains like quinoa or oats with toppings such as fresh fruits, nuts, seeds, and a drizzle of maple syrup or plant-based yogurt. These breakfast bowls provide a satisfying and nutritious start to your morning.

Legume-based Pancakes: Create fluffy and protein-packed pancakes by using legume-based flours like chickpea or lentil flour. These flours add a nutty flavor and a boost of nutrients to your breakfast. Serve them with a dollop of nut butter, fresh berries, or a sprinkle of seeds for added texture and flavor.

Seed Porridge: Experiment with seed-based porridge by blending a combination of chia seeds, flaxseeds, and hemp seeds with plant-based milk, sweeteners like dates or maple syrup, and flavorings such as cinnamon or vanilla extract. Let the mixture sit overnight to allow the seeds to absorb the liquid, resulting in a creamy and nutritious breakfast porridge.

Section 13: Global Inspirations: Grains, Legumes, and Seeds in International Cuisine

Middle Eastern-Inspired Quinoa Tabouli: Give the traditional tabouli salad a twist by substituting bulgur wheat with quinoa. Toss cooked quinoa with finely chopped fresh vegetables like tomatoes, cucumbers, onions, parsley, mint, lemon juice, and olive oil. This refreshing salad is packed with nutrients and offers a modern take on a classic dish.

Indian-Inspired Lentil Dal: Experience the rich flavors of Indian cuisine with a comforting lentil dal. Sauté onions, garlic, ginger, and spices in oil, then add cooked lentils and simmer until well combined. Serve with basmati rice, poppadums or naan bread for a complete and satisfying meal.

Mexican-Inspired Black Bean and Corn Salad: Create a vibrant and flavorful salad by combining cooked black beans, sweet corn, diced tomatoes, bell peppers, red onions, and fresh cilantro. Dress the salad with lime juice, olive oil, cumin, and chili powder for a Mexican-inspired delight. Enjoy it as a side dish or as a filling for tacos or burritos.

Proper Storage: To maintain the freshness and nutritional value of grains, legumes, and seeds, it's important to store them properly. Keep them in airtight containers in a cool, dry, and dark place. This helps prevent moisture, heat, and light from causing spoilage or nutrient degradation. Labeling the containers with the purchase date can help you keep track of their freshness.

Bulk Buying: Consider purchasing grains, legumes, and seeds in bulk to reduce packaging waste and save money. Many stores offer bulk sections where you can fill your own reusable containers. This allows you to buy the quantities you need while minimizing environmental impact.

Upcycling Leftovers: If you find yourself with leftover cooked grains, legumes, or seeds, don't let them go to waste. They can be repurposed into new dishes. For example, use cooked grains in soups, salads, or stir-fries, or blend them into patties for veggie burgers. Leftover legumes can be mashed and used as a base for dips or spreads.

Section 14: Exploring Cultural Traditions and Adaptations

Ancient Grains: Discover the diverse array of ancient grains from different cultures, such as amaranth, teff, or spelt. These grains offer unique flavors, textures, and nutritional profiles.

International Legume Dishes: Explore traditional legume-based dishes from various cuisines, such as Indian dal, Ethiopian lentil stews, or Mexican refried beans. Adapt these recipes to incorporate your favorite legumes and experiment with spices and seasonings to create exciting flavor profiles.

Seed-Based Condiments: Experiment with seed-based condiments like tahini, sunflower seed butter, or pumpkin seed pesto. These flavorful additions can be used as spreads, dressings, or toppings to elevate the taste and nutritional value of your meals.

Section 15: The Art of Seasoning with Herbs, Spices, and Seasonings

Understanding Flavor Profiles: Herbs, spices, and seasonings offer a vast array of flavors that can elevate your dishes. Familiarize yourself with different flavor profiles, such as warm and earthy, fresh and citrusy, or spicy and aromatic. Experiment with combining herbs and spices to create unique flavor combinations that suit your taste preferences.

Fresh Herbs: Incorporate fresh herbs into your cooking for a burst of vibrant flavor. Common herbs like basil, parsley, cilantro, and mint can add brightness and freshness to salads, soups, sauces, and marinades. Chop them finely and add them toward the end of cooking to preserve their delicate flavors.

Dried Herbs: Dried herbs offer convenience and long shelf life while still imparting delicious flavors. They are perfect for adding depth to soups, stews, sauces, and roasted vegetables. Remember that dried herbs are more potent than fresh ones, so use them sparingly and adjust the amount to your taste. If you have a green thumb, you can try growing herbs on a windowsill in your house to ensure you always have access to a variety of herbs.

Spice Blends: Explore the world of spice blends from different cuisines, such as garam masala, curry powder, Italian seasoning, or Chinese five-spice. These pre-mixed spice blends offer a convenient way to add complex flavors to your dishes. Experiment with homemade spice blends to customize the flavor profiles to your liking.

Section 16: Enhancing Culinary Techniques with Herbs, Spices, and Seasonings

Infusing Flavors: Infuse your cooking oils or plant-based butters with herbs and spices to add depth and aroma. Heat the oil or butter gently with your chosen herbs and spices, then strain out the solids for a flavorful base for sautéing, roasting, or dressings.

Marinating: Create complex-tasting marinades by combining herbs, spices, citrus juices, and plant-based oils. Marinating allows the flavors to penetrate and tenderize the ingredients, resulting in more flavorful and succulent dishes. Experiment with different combinations to create your signature marinades.

Dry Rubs and Spice Mixes: Enhance the flavor of your grilled or roasted dishes by using dry rubs and spice mixes. These blends typically include a combination of herbs, spices, salt, and pepper. Massage the mixture onto the surface of the ingredients before cooking to infuse them with robust flavors.

Balancing Flavors: When using herbs, spices, and seasonings, it's crucial to achieve a balance of flavors. Experiment with the right amount of sweet, sour, salty, and spicy elements to create well-rounded dishes. It's so important that you taste as you cook and adjust as needed to ensure harmony in your flavors.

Emerald Apron

Section 17: Exploring Cultural Culinary Traditions

Indian Spices: Dive into the vibrant world of Indian cuisine and explore spices like cumin, coriander, turmeric, cardamom, and garam masala. These spices create complex flavors and aromatic dishes. Learn traditional Indian cooking techniques, such as tempering spices in hot oil, to unlock the full potential of these flavors.

Mediterranean Herbs: Experience the flavors of the Mediterranean with herbs like oregano, thyme, rosemary, and basil. These herbs are commonly used in dishes from Greece, Italy, and the Middle East, imparting a unique and aromatic character. Combine them with olive oil, lemon juice, and garlic for a taste of the Mediterranean.

Asian Aromatics: Asian cuisines feature an array of aromatic ingredients like ginger, garlic, lemongrass, and chili peppers. These ingredients add depth and complexity to dishes, whether it's stir-fries, curries, or soups. Learn about the art of balancing sweet, sour, salty, and spicy flavors in Asian cooking.

Chapter 8 has taken us on a rich and insightful journey into the realm of grains, legumes, and seeds. We have explored their nutritional benefits, learned various cooking techniques, and discovered creative ways to incorporate them into our plant-based meals. These nutrient-rich staples have shown us their versatility, flavor profiles, and immense potential for nourishing our bodies.

By embracing the power of grains, legumes, and seeds, we have unlocked a world of culinary possibilities. We have witnessed how these humble ingredients can transform into hearty grain bowls, comforting stews, and delectable desserts. Their abundance of protein, fiber, vitamins, minerals, and antioxidants contribute to a balanced and wholesome plant-based diet.

Throughout this chapter, we have seen the importance of sustainable sourcing, choosing organic and fair-trade options whenever possible. By supporting local farmers and opting for heirloom varieties, we not only prioritize our health but also contribute to a more sustainable and environmentally friendly food system.

Proper storage techniques have also been emphasized to preserve the freshness and nutritional value of grains, legumes, and seeds. By keeping them in airtight containers, away from heat, moisture, and light, we ensure that these valuable ingredients retain their quality and maximize their benefits.

Additionally, we have explored cultural culinary traditions and adaptations, broadening our understanding of global cuisines and incorporating diverse flavors into our plant-based meals. From Indian spices to Mediterranean herbs, we have embraced the richness and depth of different culinary traditions, adding a world of taste and aroma to our cooking.

Emerald Apron

Chapter 9

Creative Substitutions: Making Plant-Based Swaps in Classic Recipes

Chapter 9 explores the art of making creative substitutions in classic recipes to transform them into delicious plant-based dishes. By replacing animal-based ingredients with plant-based alternatives, we can enjoy familiar flavors while challenging our cooking skills and inventing new recipes for our repertoire.. This chapter will provide insights into various plant-based swaps and offer guidance on adapting traditional recipes to suit a plant-based diet.

Section 1: Plant-Based Dairy Substitutes

Non-Dairy Milks: Discover the wide variety of non-dairy milk options, such as almond, soy, oat, and coconut milk. Learn about their unique flavors, textures, and culinary applications, including their use in baking, cooking, and beverages.

Plant-Based Creams and Butters: Explore alternatives to dairy-based creams and butters, such as coconut cream, cashew cream, and avocado as a butter substitute. These options provide richness, creaminess, and functionality in recipes.

Vegan Cheese: Delve into the world of vegan cheese, which offers a range of flavors and textures. Learn about nut-based cheeses, tofu-based options, and the art of making homemade vegan cheese to add a savory element to your dishes.

Section 2: Plant-Based Egg Replacements

Flaxseed and Chia seeds: Discover the binding properties of flaxseeds and chia seeds, which can be used as egg replacements in baking and cooking. Learn how to prepare these simple and effective substitutes and adapt them to various recipes.

Aquafaba: Uncover the magic of aquafaba, the liquid found in canned chickpeas, which can be whipped and used as an egg white replacement. Explore its versatility in creating meringues, macarons, mousses, and more.

Tofu and Silken Tofu: Harness the versatility of tofu as an egg substitute in recipes that require structure and moisture. Silken tofu, in particular, works well in custards, puddings, and creamy desserts.

Section 3: Plant-Based Meat Alternatives

Mushrooms: Mushrooms are such an underrated vegetable – they are a delicious addition to stews, casseroles curries and stirfrys. They are also available cheaply in most parts of the world and are a great source of healthy gut biomes.

Jackfruit: This sweet fruit has a rich and subtle flavor which resembles meat. It has an incredible amount of health benefits, from its antioxidant properties to providing you with vitamin A. Jackfruit is delicious as a meat-substitute in tacos, curries and burgers.

Section 4: Plant-Based Sweeteners

Natural Sweeteners: Explore a range of natural sweeteners, such as maple syrup, agave nectar, coconut sugar, and date paste. Learn about their flavors, sweetness levels, and how to incorporate them into baking, desserts, and beverages.

Fruit Purees: Discover the natural sweetness and moisture provided by fruit purees, such as applesauce, mashed bananas, and pumpkin puree. Learn how to use these alternatives in place of traditional sweeteners in baking and desserts.

Stevia and Monk Fruit: Explore zero-calorie sweeteners like stevia and monk fruit, which offer sweetness without the added sugar. Learn about their unique properties and how to use them in moderation to achieve desired sweetness.

Section 5: Plant-Based Fats and Oils

Healthy Cooking Oils: Discover plant-based cooking oils that offer a balance of flavor and health benefits. Olive oil, avocado oil, coconut oil, and sesame oil are just a few examples. Learn about their smoke points, ideal uses, and how to incorporate them into cooking and baking.

Nut and Seed Butters: Embrace the richness and creaminess of nut and seed butters as alternatives to dairy-based spreads and ingredients. Peanut butter, almond butter, tahini, and sunflower seed butter provide not only flavor but also essential fats, protein, and other nutrients.

Avocado: Harness the versatility of avocados as a plant-based fat source. From creamy dressings and spreads to baked goods and smoothies, avocados offer a unique texture and healthy fats that contribute to satiety and a nourishing diet.

Section 6: Plant-Based Flavor Enhancers

Vegetable Broths and Stocks: Replace traditional meat-based broths and stocks with flavorful vegetable versions. Create your own homemade vegetable broth or explore store-bought options to enhance the taste of soups, stews, and sauces.

Tamari and Liquid Aminos: Discover gluten-free alternatives to soy sauce, such as tamari and liquid aminos. These savory condiments add depth of flavor to stir-fries, marinades, and dressings while catering to dietary preferences and restrictions.

Nutritional Yeast: Embrace the cheesy and nutty flavors of nutritional yeast, a popular plant-based seasoning. Sprinkle it on popcorn, pasta dishes, or roasted vegetables for a boost of umami and a dairy-free alternative to Parmesan cheese.

Section 7: Adapting Traditional Recipes

Recipe Analysis: Learn how to analyze traditional recipes and identify animal-based ingredients that can be replaced with plant-based alternatives. Consider the purpose of each ingredient and its role in the recipe to make informed substitutions.

Texture and Structure: Understand the importance of texture and structure in recipes and explore plant-based ingredients that can provide similar qualities. For example, mashed bananas or applesauce can replace eggs in baking to add moisture and bind ingredients.

Flavor Balance: Consider how plant-based substitutes may affect the overall flavor profile of a dish and make adjustments to maintain balance. Experiment with herbs, spices, and seasonings to enhance the flavors and create a satisfying plant-based version.

Section 8: Plant-Based Baking Techniques

Egg Replacements in Baking: Dive deeper into the world of egg replacements in baking. Explore options like applesauce, mashed bananas, silken tofu, and flaxseed or chia seed "eggs" to achieve moisture, binding, and leavening properties in your baked goods.

Vegan Butter and Margarine: Discover plant-based alternatives to traditional butter and margarine. Vegan butter and margarine options are available in many stores, offering the same creamy texture and fat content for baking and cooking purposes.

Alternative Milk in Baking: Explore the use of plant-based milks in baking, such as almond milk, soy milk, or oat milk. Each milk alternative has its unique flavor and consistency, which can influence the overall taste and texture of baked goods.

Section 9: Plant-Based Substitutions in Savory Dishes

Vegetable Broths and Stocks: Replace meat-based broths and stocks with flavorful vegetable versions in savory dishes like soups, stews, and risottos. Homemade vegetable broth or store-bought options can impart depth and complexity to your dishes.

Plant-Based Meat Alternatives: Discover the wide range of plant-based meat alternatives available, such as tempeh, seitan, tofu, or textured vegetable protein (TVP). Experiment with these substitutes in classic recipes like lasagna, chili, or stir-fries to achieve similar textures and flavors.

Vegetable and Mushroom Substitutions: Explore the versatility of vegetables and mushrooms as replacements for meat in savory dishes. For example, cauliflower can mimic the texture of chicken, and mushrooms can add a rich umami flavor to pasta sauces or burgers.

Section 10: Adapting Ethnic and International Cuisine

Plant-Based Asian Cuisine: Adapt classic Asian dishes like stir-fries, curries, and sushi rolls to be plant-based by substituting meat with tofu, tempeh, or mushrooms. Experiment with traditional Asian seasonings like soy sauce, ginger, and garlic to enhance flavors.

Mediterranean and Middle Eastern Delights: Explore the flavors of the Mediterranean and Middle East by substituting meat with legumes like chickpeas, lentils, or falafel. Create flavorful dishes like tabbouleh, hummus, or stuffed peppers using plant-based ingredients.

Latin American and Mexican Fare: Discover the vibrancy of Latin American and Mexican cuisine with plant-based alternatives. Use beans, lentils, or grilled vegetables as substitutes in dishes like tacos, enchiladas, or rice and bean bowls for a satisfying and nutritious meal.

Section 11: Comfort Foods Reinvented

Plant-Based Mac and Cheese: Experience the creamy goodness of plant-based mac and cheese by using dairy-free cheese alternatives made from nuts, soy, or potatoes. You can combine them with nutritional yeast, plant-based milk, and spices for a comforting and indulgent dish.

Plant-Based Burgers and Sandwiches: Create flavorful and satisfying burgers and sandwiches using plant-based patties made from ingredients like beans, lentils, quinoa, or mushrooms. Load them up with fresh vegetables, condiments, and plant-based spreads for a mouthwatering meal.

Plant-Based Pizza: Enjoy a plant-powered twist on pizza by using a variety of vegetable toppings, plant-based cheeses, and tomato-based sauces. Experiment with different crusts like cauliflower, whole wheat, or gluten-free options for a wholesome and delicious pizza experience.

Section 12: Family-Friendly Favorites

Plant-Based Tacos and Burritos: Gather the family for a fiesta with plant-based tacos and burritos. Fill them with seasoned black beans, grilled vegetables, salsa, guacamole, and plant-based sour cream for a tasty and nutritious meal that everyone will enjoy.

Plant-Based Spaghetti Bolognese: Put a plant-based spin on this classic Italian dish by using lentils, mushrooms, or textured vegetable protein (TVP) in place of ground meat. Use with a rich tomato sauce, herbs, and spices for a satisfying and family-friendly pasta experience.

Plant-Based Pancakes and Waffles: Start the day off right with fluffy and delicious plant-based pancakes and waffles. Use plant-based milk, flaxseed or chia seed "eggs," and whole grain flour for a wholesome and invigorating breakfast treat. Top with fresh fruits, maple syrup, or plant-based yogurt for added indulgence.

Section 13: Holiday and Special Occasion Fare

Plant-Based Thanksgiving Feast: Celebrate the holidays with a plant-based Thanksgiving feast. Roast a stuffed butternut squash, create a lentil-based loaf, and prepare savory sides like mashed potatoes, roasted vegetables, and cranberry sauce. Finish with a plant-based pumpkin pie for a complete and satisfying holiday meal.

Plant-Based Celebration Cakes: Impress your guests with stunning plant-based celebration cakes. Explore recipes using plant-based ingredients like aquafaba or applesauce for moisture, and plant-based buttercream for frosting. Decorate with fresh fruits, edible flowers, or vegan chocolate for a show-stopping dessert.

Plant-Based Party Appetizers: Entertain guests with an array of plant-based party appetizers. Create savory dips, vegan cheese platters, stuffed mushrooms, or mini plant-based sliders for a crowd-pleasing spread that highlights the deliciousness of plant-based ingredients.

Section 14: Everyday Plant-Based Meals

Quick and Easy Weeknight Dinners: Discover a variety of plant-based meals that can be prepared in no time. From stir-fries and grain bowls to pasta dishes and sheet pan meals, these recipes will help you create satisfying and nutritious dinners for busy weekdays.

Salads and Power Bowls: Dive into the world of vibrant and nutrient-packed salads and power bowls. Experiment with different combinations of fresh vegetables, grains, legumes, and dressings to create delicious and satisfying meals that nourish your body.

Sandwiches and Wraps: Elevate your lunchtime with plant-based sandwiches and wraps. Load them with colorful vegetables, plant-based proteins, spreads, and condiments to create a satisfying and portable meal.

Section 15: Plant-Based Breakfast and Brunch Ideas

Smoothie Bowls and Overnight Oats: Start your day with refreshing and nourishing smoothie bowls or prepare overnight oats for a convenient grab-and-go breakfast. Customize them with your favorite fruits, nuts, seeds, and plant-based milk for a delicious and energizing start to your day.

Plant-Based Pancakes and Waffles: Indulge in fluffy and flavorful plant-based pancakes and waffles for a weekend brunch treat. Explore different variations using whole grains, fruits, spices, and plant-based yogurt or syrup as toppings.

Tofu Scrambles and Breakfast Burritos: Enjoy a hearty and satisfying plant-based breakfast with tofu scrambles and breakfast burritos. Season tofu with spices and vegetables to create a delicious and protein-packed scramble, or wrap it in a tortilla with beans, vegetables, and plant-based cheese for a portable morning meal.

Section 16: Snacks and Appetizers

Plant-Based Energy Balls and Bars: Whip up homemade energy balls and bars using nuts, seeds, dried fruits, and natural sweeteners. These portable snacks provide a quick boost of energy and are perfect for on-the-go or post-workout refueling.

Veggie Dips and Spreads: Create flavorful and nutritious veggie dips and spreads using plant-based ingredients like beans, avocado, or roasted vegetables. Pair them with fresh-cut vegetables, whole-grain crackers, or bread for a satisfying and healthy snack.

Plant-Based Sweets and Treats: Indulge your sweet tooth with plant-based sweets and treats. From bliss balls and fruit-based desserts to homemade granola bars and cookies, there are endless options to satisfy your cravings in a healthier way.

Section 17: Plant-Based Beverages

Smoothies and Juices: Explore a variety of plant-based smoothies and juices that are not only refreshing but also packed with vitamins, minerals, and antioxidants. Blend together a combination of fruits, leafy greens, plant-based milk, and optional add-ins like nut butter or chia seeds for a nutritious and satisfying drink.

Herbal Teas and Infusions: Embrace the comforting and healing properties of herbal teas and infusions. Discover the wide range of flavors and benefits offered by herbs like chamomile, peppermint, ginger, or hibiscus, and learn how to prepare soothing hot or refreshing iced beverages.

Plant-Based Mocktails: Celebrate special occasions or simply indulge in a delicious and alcohol-free plant-based mocktail. Experiment with different fruit juices, sparkling water, herbs, and garnishes to create refreshing and visually appealing beverages for any gathering.

Section 18: Plant-Based Condiments and Dressings

Homemade Nut Butters and Spreads: Take your condiments to the next level by making your own homemade nut butters and spreads. Blend your favorite nuts or seeds with a touch of sweetness, spices, or savory flavors for a delightful and customizable addition to your meals. Hummus made with chickpeas is another tasty and easy dip – it's especially perfect for wraps and falafel.

Fresh and Flavorful Dressings: It is so easy to make yummy plant-based dressings with ingredients like balsamic dressing, cajun spice and citrus juices. Mix together ingredients like citrus juices, vinegar, herbs, and plant-based yogurt or tahini for a burst of flavor that complements your greens and veggies. These work great on burgers, salads or mezze plates.

Dips and Sauces: Amp up the taste of your snacks and meals with a variety of plant-based dips and sauces. From guacamole and hummus to salsa and tahini-based sauces,

Emerald Apron

Chapter 10

Quick and Easy Weeknight Meals for Busy Plant-Based Enthusiasts

Life can get hectic, and finding the time to prepare healthy and delicious meals on busy weeknights can feel like a daunting task. But fear not! In Chapter 10 of "The Green Apron: Plant-Based Made Easy," we have curated a collection of quick and easy weeknight meals that are perfect for busy plant-based enthusiasts like you. These recipes are designed to help you whip up nourishing and satisfying meals in a flash, without compromising on taste or nutrition. Whether you're a working professional, a busy parent, or someone with a packed schedule, these recipes will be your go-to resource for creating hassle-free plant-based meals that fit seamlessly into your busy lifestyle.

Section 1: Speedy Stir-Fries and Sautéed Delights

Techniques: Master the art of quick stir-fries and sautés with these simple techniques:

Preparing Ingredients: Begin by chopping your vegetables and protein sources into bite-sized pieces for even and quick cooking. Marinate tofu or tempeh in flavorful sauces to infuse them with taste.

High Heat Cooking: Heat a wok or skillet on high heat and add a small amount of oil. Quickly stir-fry your vegetables, allowing them to retain their vibrant colors and crisp texture.

Mouth-watering Sauces: Whip up delicious stir-fry sauces by combining soy sauce, ginger, garlic, and a touch of sweetness. Toss your cooked vegetables and proteins in the sauce to coat them evenly.

Handful of Ingredients: Create stir-fries and sautés with these versatile ingredients:

Colorful Vegetables: Bell peppers, broccoli, carrots, snap peas, and mushrooms add vibrant colors and a variety of textures to your dishes.

Protein Sources: Tofu, tempeh, seitan, or edamame are excellent plant-based proteins that absorb flavors and provide a satisfying texture.

Aromatics: Garlic, ginger, and scallions add depth and fragrance to your stir-fries and sautés.

Section 2: Effortless Pasta and Noodle Creations

Techniques: Speed up your pasta and noodle dishes with these techniques:

Boiling Pasta: Cook your pasta according to package instructions until al dente. Drain and set aside, reserving some of the cooking water to adjust the sauce consistency.

Quick Sauces: Prepare quick and flavorful sauces by combining ingredients like crushed tomatoes, herbs, spices, and plant-based cream substitutes. Simmer the sauce briefly to allow the flavors to meld together.

Stir-frying Noodles: Use high heat to stir-fry your cooked noodles with vegetables and sauces. Toss them quickly to prevent sticking and ensure even distribution of flavors.

Handful of Ingredients: Create delicious pasta and noodle dishes with these key ingredients:

Pasta Varieties: Choose whole grain or gluten-free pasta options like spaghetti, penne, or fusilli.

Sauce Bases: Tomatoes, plant-based cream substitutes, and vegetable broths form the foundation of your pasta and noodle sauces.

Flavor Enhancers: Garlic, onions, herbs like basil and oregano, and spices like red pepper flakes or curry powder add depth and complexity to your dishes.

Section 3: Sheet Pan Wonders: One-Pan Meals

Techniques: Simplify your cooking process with these sheet pan techniques:

Preparing Ingredients: Cut your vegetables and protein sources into even-sized pieces for consistent cooking. Coat them with oil, herbs, and spices for enhanced flavors.

Arranging on the Pan: Spread out the ingredients evenly on a sheet pan, making sure to leave space between them for proper browning and crispness.

Roasting Temperatures: Preheat your oven to the recommended temperature and roast the ingredients until tender and lightly browned. Flip or stir them halfway through the cooking process for even browning.

Handful of Ingredients: Create delicious sheet pan meals with these versatile ingredients:

Colorful Vegetables: Bell peppers, zucchini, sweet potatoes, cauliflower, and Brussels sprouts offer a variety of flavors and textures.

Protein Sources: Chickpeas, tofu, tempeh, or plant-based sausages can serve as the star protein of your sheet pan meals.

Seasonings: Experiment with herbs, spices, and condiments like garlic, paprika, cumin, balsamic vinegar, or soy sauce to elevate the flavors of your sheet pan creations.

Section 4: Wholesome Grain Bowls: Easy and Nutritious

Techniques: Master the art of assembling wholesome grain bowls with these techniques:

Cooking Grains: Follow the instructions on the package to cook your grains to perfection. Fluff them with a fork and let them cool slightly before assembling your bowls.

Layering Ingredients: Start with a base of cooked grains, followed by protein sources, vegetables, and toppings. Arrange them beautifully for a visually appealing presentation.

Drizzling Dressings: Prepare flavorful dressings by combining ingredients like olive oil, vinegar, citrus juice, herbs, and spices. Drizzle the dressing over the assembled grain bowl just before serving to enhance the flavors.

Handful of Ingredients: Create nourishing grain bowls with these essential ingredients:

Whole Grains: Choose from a variety of options such as brown rice, quinoa, farro, barley, or couscous.

Protein Sources: Include beans, lentils, tofu, tempeh, or grilled plant-based meats for a protein-rich component.

Colorful Vegetables: Add a mix of fresh or roasted vegetables like leafy greens, cherry tomatoes, cucumber, roasted sweet potatoes, and roasted bell peppers.

Section 5: Speedy and Flavorful Salads

Techniques: Whip up quick and flavorful salads with these techniques:

Fresh Ingredients: Choose crisp and vibrant leafy greens, herbs, and vegetables. Wash and dry them thoroughly to retain their freshness and crunch.

Prepping Ahead: Wash and chop your vegetables in advance for quick assembly. Store them in airtight containers to maintain their freshness.

Dressing Distribution: Toss your salad with the dressing just before serving to evenly coat the ingredients and prevent the greens from wilting.

Handful of Ingredients: Create refreshing and flavorful salads with these essential ingredients:

Leafy Greens: Opt for lettuce, spinach, kale, arugula, or mixed greens as the base of your salad.

Colorful Vegetables: Include cucumbers, tomatoes, carrots, bell peppers, radishes, or avocados for added crunch and vibrancy.

Toppings and Dressings: Add nuts, seeds, dried fruits, croutons, or homemade dressings for a burst of flavor and texture.

Section 6: Express Soups and Stews

Techniques: Prepare quick and comforting soups and stews with these techniques:

Sautéing Aromatics: Start by sautéing onions, garlic, and other aromatics in a pot to release their flavors and create a flavorful base for your soup or stew.

Simmering and Seasoning: Add your choice of vegetables, protein sources, broth, and seasonings to the pot and simmer until all the flavors meld together.

Blending or Thickening: Use an immersion blender or a countertop blender to blend the ingredients for a smooth soup. Alternatively, use cornstarch or arrowroot powder as a thickening agent for heartier stews.

Handful of Ingredients: Create delicious soups and stews with these essential ingredients:

Broths: Choose vegetable or mushroom broth as the base for your soups and stews.

Vegetables: Include a variety of seasonal vegetables like carrots, celery, potatoes, tomatoes, and leafy greens.

Protein Sources: Add beans, lentils, tempeh, tofu, or plant-based meat substitutes for a protein-packed soup or stew.

Section 7: Speedy and Satisfying Sandwiches and Wraps

Techniques:

Flavorful Spreads: Create delicious spreads like hummus, pesto, or tahini sauce to enhance the taste of your sandwiches and wraps.

Proper Layering: Start with a sturdy bread or wrap, layer with proteins, vegetables, and spreads, and finish with leafy greens or fresh herbs for added crunch and freshness.

Wrapping Techniques: Master the art of wrapping your sandwiches or rolls tightly to prevent fillings from falling out while eating.

Handful of Ingredients:

Breads and Wraps: Choose from whole wheat bread, ciabatta, pita, tortillas, or lettuce wraps as the base for your sandwiches and wraps.

Proteins: Use plant-based proteins like grilled tofu, tempeh, falafel, or marinated portobello mushrooms as the star of your sandwich or wrap.

Fresh Vegetables: Add a variety of vegetables such as sliced tomatoes, lettuce, cucumber, bell peppers, and sprouts for a refreshing crunch.

Flavor Boosters: Amp up the flavors with ingredients like avocado, pickles, olives, roasted red peppers, or spicy condiments like sriracha or mustard.

Section 8: Quick and Flavorful Pizza and Flatbreads

Techniques:

Pre-made Pizza Dough: Save time by using store-bought or pre-made pizza dough, or make your own ahead of time.

Flavorful Sauces: Explore various pizza sauces such as tomato-based marinara, pesto, or garlic-infused olive oil for added flavor.

Toppings and Cheeses: Experiment with a variety of toppings like fresh vegetables, plant-based cheeses, herbs, and spices for a personalized touch.

Handful of Ingredients:

Pizza Dough: Choose from store-bought or homemade pizza dough to create the perfect crust.

Sauce Options: Tomato-based marinara, creamy vegan Alfredo, or pesto sauces offer a variety of flavor profiles for your pizzas and flatbreads.

Vegetable Toppings: Bell peppers, onions, mushrooms, spinach, cherry tomatoes, and artichoke hearts add color and texture to your pizzas.

Plant-Based Cheeses: Explore options like vegan mozzarella, cashew-based ricotta, or homemade nut-based cheeses for a cheesy and melty texture.

Section 9: Express Grain-Free Meals

Techniques:

Vegetable Substitutions: Replace traditional grains with vegetables like cauliflower rice, zucchini noodles, or spaghetti squash for a grain-free alternative.

Quick Sauté: Stir-fry your vegetables with spices and seasonings to enhance their flavors and mimic the texture of traditional grains.

Creative Combining: Combine different vegetables and protein sources to create a satisfying and nutrient-rich grain-free meal.

Handful of Ingredients:

Cauliflower: Process cauliflower florets in a food processor to create a rice-like texture or use it as a base for grain-free pizza crusts.

Zucchini: Spiralize or julienne zucchini to make noodles or use them as a replacement for lasagna sheets in a grain-free lasagna.

Spaghetti Squash: Roast or steam spaghetti squash, then scrape the flesh with a fork to create long, noodle-like strands.

Protein Sources: Include tofu, tempeh, chickpeas, or lentils to add a protein component to your grain-free meals.

Flavor Enhancers: Use herbs, spices, and sauces like soy sauce, nutritional yeast, garlic powder, or tahini to elevate the flavors of your grain-free creations.

Section 10: Wholesome and Speedy Tofu and Tempeh Recipes

Techniques:

Pressing Tofu: Pressing tofu helps remove excess moisture and allows it to absorb marinades and sauces better. Wrap the tofu in a kitchen towel and place a heavy object on top to squeeze out the moisture.

Marinating: Let tofu or tempeh marinate in a flavorful sauce or seasoning blend to infuse them with taste and enhance their texture.

Various Cooking Methods: Experiment with baking, stir-frying, grilling, or pan-frying tofu and tempeh to achieve different textures and flavors.

Handful of Ingredients:

Tofu: Firm or extra-firm tofu is perfect for stir-frying, grilling, or baking. Silken tofu is suitable for blending into creamy sauces or desserts.

Tempeh: This fermented soy product has a nutty flavor and firm texture, making it ideal for marinating and grilling or baking.

Marinades and Sauces: Use soy sauce, tamari, teriyaki sauce, BBQ sauce, or a homemade marinade with herbs and spices to flavor your tofu or tempeh.

Seasonings and Spices: Experiment with garlic powder, onion powder, smoked paprika, cumin, or chili flakes to enhance the flavors of your tofu or tempeh dishes.

Section 11: 30-Minute or Less Indian-Inspired Curries

Techniques:

Prepping Ingredients: Chop onions, garlic, and ginger ahead of time to save cooking time. Use pre-made curry powder or make a batch of homemade spice blends in advance.

One-Pot Cooking: Prepare curries in a single pot to minimize clean-up and make the cooking process more efficient.

Quick Simmering: Allow the flavors to meld together by simmering the curry for a short period, ensuring that the vegetables are cooked but still retain their texture.

Handful of Ingredients:

Curry Base: Use a combination of onions, garlic, ginger, and spices like turmeric, cumin, coriander, and garam masala to create a flavorful curry base.

Protein Sources: Chickpeas, lentils, tofu, or vegetables like potatoes and cauliflower can be used as the main protein component in your Indian-inspired curries.

Creamy Additions: Coconut milk, cashew cream, or dairy-free yogurt can be added to create a creamy and rich texture in your curries.

Fresh Herbs and Garnishes: Fresh cilantro, mint, or lime juice provide a burst of freshness and enhance the flavors of your Indian-inspired curries.

Section 12: Speedy Mexican-Inspired Favorites

Techniques:

Quick Salsas: Prepare fresh salsas using ripe tomatoes, onions, cilantro, lime juice, and optional jalapeños for a burst of flavor.

Flavorful Seasonings: Use a combination of spices like cumin, chili powder, paprika, and oregano to infuse Mexican-inspired dishes with rich and aromatic flavors.

Assembly Techniques: Master the art of assembling tacos, burritos, and enchiladas by layering ingredients in a way that ensures even distribution of flavors.

Handful of Ingredients:

Tortillas: Choose corn or flour tortillas as the base for your tacos, burritos, and quesadillas.

Beans: Include black beans, pinto beans, or refried beans to add protein and texture to your Mexican-inspired dishes.

Fresh Vegetables: Opt for ingredients like tomatoes, lettuce, avocados, onions, and bell peppers to provide freshness and crunch.

Mexican Cheeses: Use plant-based versions of traditional Mexican cheeses like queso fresco or Cotija for added creaminess and flavor.

Toppings and Salsas: Experiment with toppings such as guacamole, salsa verde, pico de gallo, or pickled jalapeños to add zing and enhance the overall taste.

Section 13: Easy and Flavorful Mediterranean-Inspired Meals

Techniques:

Marinating: Marinate proteins like tofu, tempeh, or vegetables in a mixture of olive oil, lemon juice, garlic, and herbs to infuse them with Mediterranean flavors.

Bright Citrus Flavors: Incorporate fresh lemon juice or zest to add brightness and tanginess to your Mediterranean dishes.

Layering Flavors: Build complex flavors by using a variety of herbs and spices like oregano, thyme, basil, rosemary, paprika, and cinnamon.

Handful of Ingredients:

Olive Oil: Use extra-virgin olive oil as the base for dressings, marinades, and sautéing to add richness and a distinct Mediterranean flavor.

Fresh Herbs: Include herbs like parsley, basil, mint, dill, and oregano for a fresh and aromatic taste.

Olives and Capers: Introduce the briny flavors of olives and capers for a distinctive Mediterranean touch.

Grains and Legumes: Incorporate ingredients like couscous, bulgur, chickpeas, lentils, or white beans to provide a hearty and nutritious element to your Mediterranean meals.

Roasted Vegetables: Roast vegetables like eggplant, zucchini, bell peppers, and cherry tomatoes to add depth and sweetness to your dishes.

Section 14: Speedy and Versatile Asian-Inspired Stir-Fries

Techniques:

High Heat Cooking: Stir-fry your ingredients quickly over high heat to retain their crispness and prevent them from becoming soggy.

Flavorful Stir-Fry Sauces: Create homemade stir-fry sauces using ingredients like soy sauce, ginger, garlic, rice vinegar, and a touch of sweetness for a balance of flavors.

Proper Ingredient Preparation: Slice vegetables and proteins into thin and uniform pieces to ensure even cooking and quick heat absorption.

Handful of Ingredients:

Rice and Noodles: Choose from options like jasmine rice, brown rice, rice noodles, or udon noodles as the base for your Asian-inspired stir-fries.

Vegetables: Include a variety of vegetables such as bok choy, bell peppers, snap peas, mushrooms, broccoli, and carrots for vibrant colors and textures.

Protein Sources: Use tofu, tempeh, seitan, or plant-based meat substitutes as a protein component in your stir-fries.

Asian Sauces and Condiments: Explore flavors with ingredients like soy sauce, hoisin sauce, sesame oil, chili paste, and oyster sauce for a depth of umami and complexity.

Garnishes: Top your stir-fries with chopped green onions, cilantro, toasted sesame seeds, or crushed peanuts for added freshness and texture.

Section 15: Quick and Satisfying Buddha Bowls

Techniques:

Grain and Protein Preparation: Cook grains like quinoa, brown rice, or farro, and prepare proteins such as roasted chickpeas or marinated tofu to be used as the base of your Buddha bowls.

Colorful Arrangement: Assemble your Buddha bowls by placing grains, proteins, and an array of colorful vegetables in an aesthetically pleasing manner.

Flavorful Dressings: Create flavorful dressings using ingredients like tahini, lemon juice, Dijon mustard, maple syrup, and spices to tie all the elements together.

Handful of Ingredients:

Grains: Choose your preferred grain, such as quinoa, brown rice, or bulgur, as the foundation of your Buddha bowl.

Proteins: Include plant-based proteins like roasted chickpeas, lentils, tempeh, or marinated tofu for a satisfying and protein-rich component.

Assorted Vegetables: Incorporate a variety of fresh or roasted vegetables like roasted sweet potatoes, steamed broccoli, cherry tomatoes, cucumbers, and shredded carrots for a colorful and nutritious bowl.

Leafy Greens: Add a bed of fresh spinach, kale, or mixed greens for an extra boost of vitamins and minerals.

Toppings and Dressings: Enhance the flavor with toppings such as avocado slices, toasted nuts or seeds, fresh herbs, and dressings like tahini sauce, lemon vinaigrette, or miso-ginger dressing.

Section 16: Speedy and Flavorful Pasta and Noodle Dishes

Techniques:

Boiling Pasta and Noodles: Cook pasta and noodles according to package instructions until al dente, then drain and rinse with cold water to stop the cooking process.

Quick Pan Sauces: Create simple pan sauces by combining ingredients like olive oil, garlic, herbs, and spices for a burst of flavor.

Tossing and Coating: Toss cooked pasta or noodles with sauces, vegetables, and proteins to evenly coat them with flavor.

Handful of Ingredients:

Pasta and Noodles: Choose from a variety of pasta shapes like spaghetti, fettuccine, penne, or linguine. Explore Asian noodles like rice noodles, soba noodles, or udon noodles.

Sauces and Flavors: Utilize marinara sauce, creamy vegan alfredo, pesto, or soy sauce-based stir-fry sauces for a range of delicious pasta and noodle dishes.

Vegetables: Incorporate vegetables such as cherry tomatoes, spinach, broccoli, mushrooms, bell peppers, or zucchini to add color, texture, and nutrients to your dishes.

Protein Sources: Add plant-based proteins like chickpeas, tofu, tempeh, or vegan meat substitutes to make your pasta or noodle dishes more filling and satisfying.

Garnishes: Sprinkle your pasta or noodle dishes with fresh herbs like basil, parsley, or cilantro, and finish with a drizzle of olive oil or a sprinkle of nutritional yeast for added flavor.

Section 17: One-Pot Meals: Quick and Easy Cleanup

Techniques:

Layering Ingredients: Add ingredients in a specific order to ensure even cooking and optimal flavors.

Simmering and Braising: Allow the ingredients to cook slowly in a single pot, allowing the flavors to meld together and creating a rich and comforting meal.

Adjusting Seasonings: Taste and adjust the seasonings as needed during the cooking process to achieve a perfectly balanced dish.

Handful of Ingredients:

Grains or Pasta: Utilize grains like rice, quinoa, or couscous, or pasta varieties like orzo or macaroni as the base of your one-pot meals.

Protein Sources: Include plant-based proteins such as beans, lentils, chickpeas, or textured vegetable protein (TVP) to provide a substantial element to your dishes.

Vegetables: Add a variety of vegetables like carrots, peas, bell peppers, onions, and celery to enhance the nutritional value and add vibrant colors to your one-pot meals.

Broths or Sauces: Use vegetable broth, tomato sauce, coconut milk, or other flavorful sauces as the liquid component to infuse your one-pot meals with delicious taste.

Herbs and Spices: Incorporate dried herbs like thyme, oregano, or rosemary, as well as spices such as paprika, cumin, or turmeric, to elevate the flavors of your one-pot creations.

Section 18: Quick and Easy Sheet Pan Meals

Techniques:

Sheet Pan Preparation: Line your sheet pan with parchment paper or foil for easy cleanup and to prevent sticking.

Uniform Cutting: Cut your ingredients into similar-sized pieces to ensure even cooking and consistent textures.

Seasoning and Spices: Use a variety of herbs, spices, and marinades to add flavor to your sheet pan meals.

Handful of Ingredients:

Protein Sources: Include plant-based proteins like tofu, tempeh, seitan, or vegan sausages to serve as the main protein component of your sheet pan meals.

Colorful Vegetables: Utilize a variety of vegetables such as bell peppers, broccoli, cauliflower, Brussels sprouts, sweet potatoes, or cherry tomatoes to create a visually appealing and nutritious sheet pan meal.

Roasting Marinades: Combine ingredients like olive oil, balsamic vinegar, garlic, lemon juice, and herbs to create flavorful marinades for your vegetables and proteins.

Garnishes: Finish your sheet pan meals with fresh herbs like parsley or basil, a sprinkle of nutritional yeast, or a drizzle of tangy sauce or dressing for added taste and presentation.

Section 19: Quick and Nourishing Breakfasts

Techniques:

Overnight Prep: Prepare overnight oats, chia seed pudding, or overnight refrigerated batters to save time in the morning.

Batch Cooking: Make large batches of granola, energy bars, or breakfast muffins in advance for quick and nutritious breakfast options throughout the week.

Smoothie Assembly: Blend together your choice of fruits, leafy greens, plant-based milk, and additional superfood boosters for a nutrient-packed morning smoothie.

Handful of Ingredients:

Oats and Grains: Use oats, quinoa, or buckwheat as the base for overnight oats, grain bowls, or breakfast porridges.

Plant-Based Milk: Choose from a variety of plant-based milks such as almond, soy, oat, or coconut to create creamy and nutritious breakfast options.

Fresh Fruits: Incorporate seasonal fruits like berries, bananas, apples, or mangoes to add natural sweetness and a burst of flavor to your breakfast creations.

Nuts and Seeds: Include almonds, walnuts, chia seeds, flaxseeds, or pumpkin seeds for added texture, healthy fats, and a nutrient boost.

Superfood Additions: Boost the nutritional value of your breakfasts with ingredients like spirulina, maca powder, cacao nibs, or hemp seeds for an extra dose of vitamins, minerals, and antioxidants.

Section 20: Speedy and Flavorful Snacks and Small Bites

Techniques:

No-Bake Energy Balls: Combine ingredients like oats, nuts, seeds, dried fruits, and nut butter to create energy-packed and easily portable snacks.

Quick Veggie Dips: Blend ingredients like Greek yogurt, tahini, lemon juice, and herbs to make flavorful and nutritious dips for fresh vegetables.

Roasting and Seasoning: Toss chickpeas, edamame, or nuts with spices and seasonings, then roast them in the oven for a crunchy and savory snack.

Assembly and Stacking: Create mini sandwiches, bruschetta, or avocado toast by stacking ingredients like vegetables, spreads, and plant-based cheeses.

Handful of Ingredients:

Nuts and Seeds: Incorporate almonds, cashews, pumpkin seeds, chia seeds, or sunflower seeds for protein, healthy fats, and a satisfying crunch.

Dried Fruits: Use dried cranberries, raisins, apricots, or dates to add natural sweetness and a chewy texture to your snacks.

Fresh Vegetables: Opt for bite-sized vegetables such as cherry tomatoes, cucumber slices, carrot sticks, or bell pepper strips for refreshing and crunchy snacks.

Whole Grain Crackers or Rice Cakes: Choose whole grain options to serve as a base for your mini sandwiches, bruschetta, or avocado toast.

Plant-Based Spreads and Dips: Explore options like hummus, guacamole, salsa, or nut-based spreads to add flavor and creaminess to your snacks.

Section 21: Quick and Energizing Smoothies and Smoothie Bowls

Techniques:

Blending Techniques: Start with a liquid base, add frozen fruits and vegetables, then blend until smooth and creamy.

Superfood Boosters: Enhance the nutritional value of your smoothies with ingredients like spirulina, chia seeds, flaxseeds, or maca powder.

Toppings and Garnishes: Add extra texture and flavor to smoothie bowls with toppings like granola, fresh fruit slices, coconut flakes, or a drizzle of nut butter.

Handful of Ingredients:

Liquid Base: Choose from plant-based milks like almond, coconut, soy, or oat milk, or use water, coconut water, or fruit juice as the base of your smoothies.

Frozen Fruits: Include a variety of frozen fruits such as berries, bananas, mangoes, pineapple, or peaches for natural sweetness and a thick and creamy texture.

Leafy Greens: Add a handful of spinach, kale, or Swiss chard to boost the nutritional value of your smoothies without altering the taste.

Protein Boost: Incorporate protein sources like silken tofu, Greek yogurt, hemp seeds, or plant-based protein powder to make your smoothies more satisfying and nourishing.

Natural Sweeteners: Use natural sweeteners like Medjool dates, honey, maple syrup, or agave nectar sparingly to add a touch of sweetness, if desired.

Section 22: Quick and Easy Desserts for Sweet Indulgences

Techniques:

No-Bake Treats: Create desserts like energy balls, raw brownies, or chia seed pudding that require no baking and can be made in minutes.

Simple Fruit Salads: Combine a variety of fresh fruits, optionally drizzled with a little honey or lemon juice, for a refreshing and light dessert.

Frozen Treats: Blend frozen fruits with plant-based milk or yogurt to make creamy and guilt-free ice cream alternatives.

Handful of Ingredients:

Dark Chocolate: Use high-quality dark chocolate with a minimum of 70% cocoa content for a rich and indulgent flavor in your desserts.

Nut Butters: Include almond butter, peanut butter, or cashew butter to add creaminess and depth of flavor to your sweet treats.

Fresh Fruits: Utilize seasonal fruits like berries, peaches, oranges, or melons to add natural sweetness and vibrancy to your desserts.

Sweeteners: Choose natural sweeteners like maple syrup, coconut sugar, or dates to sweeten your desserts in a healthier way.

Spices and Extracts: Enhance the flavors of your desserts with spices like cinnamon, nutmeg, or cardamom, or use extracts such as vanilla or almond for an extra touch of aroma.

With a focus on efficiency, flavor, and nutrition, this chapter has explored a variety of culinary techniques, ingredients, and recipes to help you create satisfying meals without compromising on taste or health.

Throughout this chapter, we have delved into the world of quick and easy weeknight meals, offering a diverse range of options to suit various tastes and preferences. From the simplicity of pasta and noodle dishes to the convenience of one-pot meals, the versatility of sheet pan dinners, and the nourishment of quick breakfast ideas, this chapter has demonstrated that plant-based cooking can be both accessible and enjoyable, even on the busiest of days.

We have explored different techniques that enable you to create mouthwatering dishes with minimal effort. Whether it's mastering the art of stir-frying, layering ingredients for one-pot meals, assembling vibrant Buddha bowls, or using sheet pans for easy cleanup, these techniques have been carefully selected to save you time and energy in the kitchen while ensuring the flavors and textures of your meals shine through.

The chapter has also highlighted a handful of key ingredients and pantry staples that form the foundation of these quick and easy weeknight meals. From grains, proteins, and vegetables to herbs, spices, and flavorful sauces, these ingredients provide a harmonious balance of taste, nutrition, and convenience, allowing you to create well-rounded and satisfying dishes in a flash.

Furthermore, the chapter has explored the importance of proper meal planning, batch cooking, and ingredient preparation to streamline your cooking process and ensure you have delicious and nutritious meals readily available throughout the week. By incorporating these strategies into your routine, you can embrace the joy of plant-based cooking while managing your time effectively.

As we conclude this chapter, we encourage you to experiment with the recipes and techniques provided, allowing your creativity to flourish in the kitchen. Remember that plant-based cooking is not only about nourishing your body but also about savoring the flavors and enjoying the process. By embracing the quick and easy weeknight meals presented in this chapter, you can confidently navigate your busy schedule while maintaining a healthy and delicious plant-based lifestyle.

Emerald Apron

Chapter 11

Indulgent Desserts: Satisfying Your Sweet Tooth the Plant-Based Way

Welcome to Chapter 11 of "The Green Apron: Plant-Based Made Easy." In this chapter, we will delve into the realm of indulgent desserts that cater to your sweet tooth while staying true to a plant-based lifestyle. Contrary to popular belief, plant-based desserts can be just as decadent, rich, and satisfying as their non-plant-based counterparts. From creamy cheesecakes to fudgy brownies, delicate pastries to luscious ice creams, we will explore a variety of desserts that will tantalize your taste buds and leave you wanting more.

In this chapter, we will not only provide you with delightful recipes but also share techniques, tips, and ingredient substitutions that will help you create indulgent plant-based desserts that are both delicious and nourishing. Whether you're a seasoned baker or a novice in the kitchen, this chapter will empower you to satisfy your cravings for sweets while embracing the benefits of a plant-based diet.

Section 1: Decadent Plant-Based Cakes and Cupcakes

Techniques:

Mixing Method: Use the creaming method or the reverse creaming method to incorporate the ingredients for a fluffy and tender cake or cupcake.

Ingredient Ratios: Understand the ratios of flour, leavening agents, fats, and liquids to ensure the perfect balance of texture and rise in your plant-based cakes and cupcakes.

Egg Replacements: Experiment with various egg substitutes like applesauce, mashed bananas, flaxseed meal, or silken tofu to bind and add moisture to your plant-based batters.

Baking Time and Temperature: Follow the recommended baking time and temperature to achieve a fully cooked cake or cupcake with a golden-brown crust.

Handful of Ingredients:

Plant-Based Milk: Choose from a variety of plant-based milks such as almond, soy, oat, or coconut milk to provide moisture and richness to your cakes and cupcakes.

Natural Sweeteners: Opt for sweeteners like maple syrup, agave nectar, or coconut sugar to add sweetness without the refined sugars often found in traditional recipes.

Vegan Butter or Oil: Use plant-based butter or oils like coconut oil, avocado oil, or vegetable oil to provide moisture and richness to your cake batters.

Flours: Explore different types of flours such as all-purpose flour, whole wheat flour, almond flour, or gluten-free flour blends to achieve the desired texture and structure in your cakes and cupcakes.

Flavor Extracts: Enhance the taste of your cakes and cupcakes with extracts like vanilla, almond, or citrus flavors to add depth and aroma.

Section 2: Creamy and Dreamy Plant-Based Cheesecakes

Techniques:

Nut-Based Crusts: Create a buttery and crumbly crust using a blend of nuts (such as almonds, walnuts, or cashews), dates, and a pinch of salt for that perfect cheesecake base.

Soaking and Blending Cashews: Soak raw cashews in water to soften them, then blend them with other ingredients like coconut cream, lemon juice, and sweeteners to achieve a creamy and smooth texture.

Baking and Chilling: Bake the cheesecake in a water bath to ensure even cooking and prevent cracking, then refrigerate for several hours or overnight to allow the flavors to develop and the cheesecake to set.

Handful of Ingredients:

Cashews: Use raw, unsalted cashews as the main ingredient for the creamy base of the cheesecake, providing a rich and luscious texture.

Coconut Cream: Incorporate full-fat coconut cream to add richness and creaminess to your plant-based cheesecakes.

Natural Sweeteners: Opt for sweeteners like agave nectar, maple syrup, or coconut sugar to add sweetness to your cheesecake without the need for refined sugars.

Lemon Juice: Add a tangy and refreshing flavor to your cheesecake with freshly squeezed lemon juice, which also helps balance the richness of the other ingredients.

Flavor Extracts: Enhance the taste of your cheesecake by adding extracts like vanilla, almond, or citrus flavors to create a delightful aroma and depth of flavor.

Section 3: Fudgy and Irresistible Plant-Based Brownies and Bars

Techniques:

Melted Chocolate: Melt vegan chocolate and combine it with other ingredients to create a rich and fudgy texture in your plant-based brownies and bars.

Egg Replacements: Experiment with substitutes like applesauce, mashed bananas, or flaxseed meal mixed with water to bind the ingredients and add moisture to your brownie or bar batter.

Mixing Method: Gently fold the dry ingredients into the wet ingredients until just combined to ensure a tender and fudgy texture in your baked treats.

Baking Time and Cooling: Bake the brownies or bars for the recommended time, then allow them to cool completely before cutting to achieve the perfect fudgy consistency.

Handful of Ingredients:

Vegan Chocolate: Choose high-quality vegan chocolate with a minimum of 70% cocoa content to provide a rich and intense chocolate flavor in your brownies and bars.

Flaxseed Meal: Use ground flaxseeds mixed with water as an egg substitute to bind the ingredients and contribute to the fudgy texture of your brownies and bars.

Natural Sweeteners: Opt for sweeteners like coconut sugar, maple syrup, or date syrup to add sweetness and depth of flavor without refined sugars.

Nuts and Nut Butters: Add chopped nuts or incorporate nut butter like almond butter or peanut butter to provide extra richness, texture, and nutty flavor to your brownies and bars.

Cocoa Powder: Use high-quality cocoa powder to intensify the chocolate flavor and deepen the color of your brownies and bars.

Section 4: Delicate and Divine Plant-Based Pastries and Pies

Techniques:

Pastry Dough: Prepare a flaky and buttery plant-based pastry dough by combining flour, plant-based butter or coconut oil, and a pinch of salt, then chilling the dough before rolling it out.

Blind Baking: Pre-bake the pastry crust before adding the filling to ensure a crisp and golden base for your plant-based pastries and pies.

Filling Preparation: Create luscious fillings by combining fruits, sweeteners, thickening agents like cornstarch or arrowroot powder, and flavorings such as lemon zest or spices.

Decorative Crusts: Explore different techniques like lattice patterns, cut-out shapes, or crimped edges to add visual appeal to your plant-based pastries and pies.

Handful of Ingredients:

Plant-Based Butter or Coconut Oil: Use plant-based butter or solid coconut oil to achieve a flaky and buttery texture in your pastry crust.

Flour: Choose all-purpose flour or a blend of all-purpose and whole wheat flour to achieve the desired texture and structure in your plant-based pastries and pies.

Seasonal Fruits: Utilize a variety of fresh fruits such as apples, berries, peaches, or pears to create vibrant and flavorful fillings for your plant-based pastries and pies.

Natural Sweeteners: Opt for sweeteners like maple syrup, coconut sugar, or agave nectar to add sweetness to your plant-based pastries and pies without relying on refined sugars.

Spices and Flavorings: Enhance the flavor profile of your pastries and pies with spices like cinnamon, nutmeg, or cardamom, or use extracts such as vanilla or almond for an extra touch of aroma.

Section 5: Wholesome and Creamy Plant-Based Ice Creams and Frozen Treats

Techniques:

Base Preparation: Blend a base of coconut milk, cashews, or frozen bananas with natural sweeteners, flavorings, and optional mix-ins to create a creamy and satisfying plant-based ice cream.

Churning: Utilize an ice cream maker to churn the ice cream base, creating a smooth and airy texture by incorporating air into the mixture.

Freezing and Ripening: After churning, transfer the ice cream to a lidded container and freeze until firm, allowing it to ripen and develop its flavors for a few hours or overnight.

Handful of Ingredients:

Coconut Milk: Use full-fat coconut milk as the main ingredient in your plant-based ice cream to provide a creamy and rich base.

Cashews: Soak raw cashews and blend them with the coconut milk for added creaminess and a smooth texture in your plant-based ice cream.

Natural Sweeteners: Opt for sweeteners like maple syrup, agave nectar, or dates to add sweetness to your ice cream while keeping it refined sugar-free.

Flavorings: Explore a variety of flavorings such as vanilla extract, cocoa powder, fruit purees, or extracts like mint or almond to create an array of delicious plant-based ice cream flavors.

Optional Mix-Ins: Enhance your ice cream with mix-ins like chocolate chips, crushed cookies, nuts, or fresh fruit chunks to add texture and additional flavor dimensions.

Section 6: Blissful and Decadent Plant-Based Dessert Sauces and Toppings

Techniques:

Reduction and Thickening: Simmer ingredients like fruits, sweeteners, and spices until they reduce and thicken, creating a luscious and syrupy dessert sauce.

Emulsification: Blend ingredients like nut butter, plant-based milk, sweeteners, and flavorings together to achieve a smooth and creamy dessert sauce or topping.

Drizzling and Pouring: Master the art of drizzling or pouring the sauce over your desserts, ensuring even distribution and a visually appealing presentation.

Handful of Ingredients:

Fruits: Utilize a variety of fruits like berries, citrus fruits, peaches, or apples to create naturally sweet and tangy dessert sauces.

Nut Butters: Incorporate almond butter, peanut butter, or cashew butter to add creaminess and depth of flavor to your sweet sauces and toppings.

Sweeteners: Choose natural sweeteners like maple syrup, coconut sugar, or dates to sweeten your sauces and toppings in a healthier way.

Spices and Extracts: Enhance the flavors of your sauces and toppings with spices like cinnamon, nutmeg, or cardamom, or use extracts such as vanilla or almond for an extra touch of aroma.

Section 7: Heavenly Plant-Based Tarts and Galettes

Techniques:

Pastry Dough: Prepare a tender and flaky plant-based pastry dough using a combination of flour, plant-based butter or coconut oil, and a pinch of salt.

Rolling and Shaping: Roll out the pastry dough into a thin, even layer and shape it into a tart pan or form rustic galette shapes.

Blind Baking: Pre-bake the pastry crust before adding the filling to ensure a crisp and golden base for your plant-based tarts and galettes.

Filling Preparation: Combine a variety of fruits, nuts, or other flavorful ingredients with natural sweeteners, thickening agents, and spices to create delicious and vibrant fillings.

Garnishing: Add an extra touch of elegance by garnishing your tarts and galettes with fresh herbs, powdered sugar, or a drizzle of plant-based cream.

Handful of Ingredients:

Plant-Based Butter or Coconut Oil: Use plant-based butter or solid coconut oil to create a flaky and buttery texture in your tart and galette crusts.

Flour: Choose all-purpose flour or a blend of all-purpose and whole wheat flour to achieve the desired texture and structure in your plant-based pastry dough.

Seasonal Fruits: Utilize a variety of fresh and ripe fruits, such as berries, stone fruits, or apples, to create vibrant and flavorful fillings for your tarts and galettes.

Natural Sweeteners: Opt for sweeteners like maple syrup, coconut sugar, or agave nectar to enhance the natural sweetness of the fruits and add depth of flavor to your fillings.

Spices and Flavorings: Experiment with spices like cinnamon, nutmeg, or cardamom, as well as flavorings such as vanilla extract or citrus zest, to elevate the flavors of your tarts and galettes.

Section 8: Wholesome and Hearty Plant-Based Crumbles and Cobblers

Techniques:

Filling Preparation: Combine your choice of fruits, natural sweeteners, thickening agents like cornstarch, and spices to create a juicy and flavorful filling for your plant-based crumbles and cobblers.

Crumble Topping: Prepare a crumbly and crunchy topping by mixing flour, oats, nuts, plant-based butter or coconut oil, and sweeteners.

Baking and Serving: Bake your crumbles and cobblers until the filling is bubbling and the topping is golden brown, then serve them warm with a scoop of plant-based ice cream or whipped coconut cream.

Handful of Ingredients:

Seasonal Fruits: Select a variety of fresh and ripe fruits, such as berries, peaches, plums, or apples, to create a naturally sweet and juicy filling for your plant-based crumbles and cobblers.

Natural Sweeteners: Use sweeteners like maple syrup, coconut sugar, or date syrup to enhance the sweetness of your fruit fillings without relying on refined sugars.

Flour: Choose all-purpose flour or whole wheat flour to create a crumbly and textured topping for your plant-based crumbles and cobblers.

Rolled Oats: Incorporate rolled oats for added texture and heartiness in the crumble topping, creating a satisfying contrast to the soft and juicy fruit filling.

Nuts: Add chopped nuts, such as almonds, walnuts, or pecans, to the crumble topping to provide a delightful crunch and nutty flavor.

Section 9: Luxurious and Silky Plant-Based Mousse and Parfaits

Techniques:

Aquafaba Whipping: Utilize the liquid from a can of chickpeas, known as aquafaba, to whip up a fluffy and stable meringue-like foam that forms the base of your plant-based mousse.

Chocolate Ganache: Create a smooth and velvety chocolate ganache by melting vegan chocolate and combining it with plant-based cream or coconut milk.

Layering and Assembly: Alternate layers of mousse, fruits, nuts, or granola to create visually appealing and delicious plant-based parfaits.

Chilling and Setting: Refrigerate your mousse or parfait for several hours or overnight to allow the flavors to develop and the texture to set.

Handful of Ingredients:

Aquafaba: Use the liquid from a can of chickpeas as an egg substitute to create a light and airy texture in your plant-based mousse.

Vegan Chocolate: Select high-quality vegan chocolate with a minimum of 70% cocoa content to provide a rich and indulgent flavor in your mousse and ganache.

Plant-Based Cream or Coconut Milk: Incorporate plant-based cream or full-fat coconut milk to add creaminess and richness to your mousse and ganache.

Fruits and Berries: Choose a variety of fresh or frozen fruits and berries to layer in your parfaits, providing a burst of freshness and natural sweetness.

Optional Toppings: Garnish your mousses and parfaits with toppings like shaved chocolate, toasted nuts, or a sprinkle of cinnamon for added texture and flavor.

Section 10: Decadent and Dreamy Plant-Based Tiramisu

Techniques:

Ladyfingers: Prepare or purchase vegan ladyfingers, a classic component of tiramisu, to provide a sponge-like texture that absorbs the coffee and liqueur flavors.

Cashew Cream: Blend soaked cashews, plant-based cream, sweeteners, and flavorings to create a luscious and creamy filling for your tiramisu layers.

Coffee Soaking: Dip the ladyfingers in a mixture of coffee and optional liqueur to infuse them with the signature flavors of tiramisu.

Layering and Chilling: Alternate layers of soaked ladyfingers and cashew cream, then refrigerate your tiramisu for a few hours or overnight to allow the flavors to meld and the dessert to set.

Handful of Ingredients:

Vegan Ladyfingers: Use vegan ladyfingers, either homemade or store-bought, to provide the structure and texture in your plant-based tiramisu.

Cashews: Soak raw cashews and blend them with plant-based cream, sweeteners, and flavorings to create a creamy and luxurious filling for your tiramisu.

Coffee and Liqueur: Brew strong coffee and optionally add a splash of liqueur like coffee liqueur, amaretto, or rum to infuse the ladyfingers with the traditional tiramisu flavors.

Cocoa Powder: Dust cocoa powder over the layers of tiramisu for a bittersweet and chocolaty element that adds depth to the dessert.

Optional Garnishes: Consider garnishing your tiramisu with grated chocolate, cocoa nibs, or a sprinkle of cinnamon for added visual appeal and flavor.

Section 11: Rich and Velvety Plant-Based Creme Brulé

Techniques:

Custard Base: Create a smooth and creamy custard base by combining plant-based milk, sweeteners, vanilla extract, and a thickening agent like cornstarch or arrowroot powder.

Baking and Chilling: Bake the custard in a water bath until set, then refrigerate for several hours or overnight to allow the flavors to develop and the creme brulee to chill.

Caramelized Sugar Topping: Sprinkle a thin layer of granulated sugar over the chilled custard, then use a kitchen torch or broiler to melt and caramelize the sugar until it forms a crispy and golden crust.

Handful of Ingredients:

Emerald Apron

Plant-Based Milk: Use a rich and creamy plant-based milk, such as coconut milk, almond milk, or soy milk, as the base for your creme brulee custard.

Natural Sweeteners: Opt for natural sweeteners like maple syrup, coconut sugar, or agave nectar to provide sweetness and depth of flavor to your custard.

Vanilla Extract: Add a hint of warmth and aroma to your creme brulee with pure vanilla extract or vanilla bean paste.

Cornstarch or Arrowroot Powder: Use a thickening agent like cornstarch or arrowroot powder to achieve the desired consistency and smooth texture in your custard.

Granulated Sugar: Sprinkle granulated sugar on top of the chilled custard for the signature caramelized crust of creme brulee.

Section 12: Decadent and Silky Plant-Based Mousse Cakes

Techniques:

Mousse Preparation: Create a velvety and airy mousse using ingredients like aquafaba, vegan chocolate, plant-based cream, and natural sweeteners.

Cake Base: Bake or assemble a plant-based cake base that serves as a sturdy foundation for your mousse layers.

Layering and Chilling: Alternate layers of mousse and cake, allowing each layer to set in the refrigerator before adding the next, creating a multi-dimensional and indulgent mousse cake.

Garnishing: Decorate the top of the mousse cake with fresh fruits, shaved chocolate, or a drizzle of chocolate ganache for an elegant and appealing presentation.

Handful of Ingredients:

Aquafaba: Utilize the liquid from a can of chickpeas as an egg white substitute to achieve a light and fluffy texture in your plant-based mousse.

Vegan Chocolate: Select high-quality vegan chocolate with a rich and smooth flavor to create the base of your mousse layers.

Plant-Based Cream: Incorporate plant-based cream or whipped coconut cream to add creaminess and richness to your mousse layers.

Natural Sweeteners: Use natural sweeteners like maple syrup, agave nectar, or coconut sugar to sweeten your mousse without the need for refined sugars.

Cake Base: Choose a plant-based cake recipe that complements the flavors of your mousse, such as chocolate, vanilla, or fruit-flavored cakes.
Section 13: Decadent and Divine Plant-Based Pies

Techniques:

Pie Crust: Prepare a flaky and buttery pie crust using plant-based butter or coconut oil, flour, and a pinch of salt, then chill the dough before rolling it out.
Filling Preparation: Create delicious fillings by combining seasonal fruits, natural sweeteners, thickening agents like cornstarch, and flavorings such as spices or extracts.
Crimping and Lattice: Decorate the edges of your pie crust by crimping them with a fork or creating a lattice pattern with strips of dough.
Baking and Cooling: Bake the pie until the crust is golden brown and the filling is bubbling, then allow it to cool completely before serving to allow the flavors to meld.
Handful of Ingredients:

Plant-Based Butter or Coconut Oil: Use plant-based butter or solid coconut oil to achieve a flaky and buttery texture in your pie crust.
Flour: Choose all-purpose flour or a blend of all-purpose and whole wheat flour to create a tender and flaky crust for your plant-based pies.
Seasonal Fruits: Select fresh and ripe fruits that are in season, such as apples, berries, peaches, or pumpkin, to create flavorful and juicy pie fillings.
Natural Sweeteners: Opt for natural sweeteners like maple syrup, coconut sugar, or date syrup to enhance the sweetness of your pie fillings without relying on refined sugars.
Spices and Flavorings: Experiment with spices like cinnamon, nutmeg, or ginger, as well as extracts such as vanilla or almond, to add depth of flavor to your plant-based pie fil
lings.
Section 14: Guilt-free and Decadent Plant-Based Cheesecakes

Techniques:

Crust Preparation: Mix together crushed cookies or nuts, plant-based butter or coconut oil, and sweetener to create a delicious and crunchy crust for your plant-based cheesecake.

Filling Creation: Blend soaked cashews or tofu with plant-based cream cheese, sweeteners, and flavorings to achieve a creamy and smooth texture for your cheesecake filling.

Baking and Cooling: Bake the cheesecake until it is set but still slightly jiggly in the center, then allow it to cool completely before refrigerating to firm up.

Topping and Garnishing: Add a variety of toppings and garnishes, such as fresh fruits, chocolate ganache, or whipped coconut cream, to enhance the flavor and presentation of your plant-based cheesecake.

Handful of Ingredients:

Cashews or Tofu: Soak raw cashews or use silken tofu as the base for your plant-based cheesecake filling, providing creaminess and a smooth texture.

Plant-Based Cream Cheese: Utilize plant-based cream cheese to add richness and tanginess to your cheesecake filling.

Sweeteners: Choose natural sweeteners like maple syrup, coconut sugar, or agave nectar to sweeten your cheesecake without relying on refined sugars.

Flavorings: Enhance the flavors of your cheesecake by adding vanilla extract, lemon zest, or extracts like almond or coconut.

Crust Ingredients: Combine crushed cookies or nuts (such as graham crackers or almonds), plant-based butter or coconut oil, and sweeteners to create a flavorful and sturdy crust for your cheesecake.

Section 15: Velvety and Creamy Plant-Based Puddings and Custards

Techniques:

Custard Base: Whisk together plant-based milk, sweeteners, thickening agents like cornstarch or arrowroot powder, and flavorings to create a smooth and velvety plant-based pudding or custard.

Cooking and Thickening: Cook the mixture over medium heat, stirring constantly, until it thickens to a pudding-like consistency.

Chilling and Setting: Pour the pudding or custard into individual serving dishes or a larger container, then refrigerate until it sets and becomes creamy and firm.

Optional Toppings: Top your pudding or custard with fresh fruits, a sprinkle of cinnamon, toasted nuts, or a dollop of plant-based whipped cream for added flavor and texture.

Handful of Ingredients:

Plant-Based Milk: Use your choice of plant-based milk, such as almond milk, oat milk, or soy milk, as the base for your pudding or custard.

Sweeteners: Select natural sweeteners like maple syrup, coconut sugar, or agave nectar to sweeten your pudding or custard without relying on refined sugars.

Thickening Agents: Incorporate cornstarch or arrowroot powder to thicken your pudding or custard and achieve a silky texture.

Flavorings: Enhance the flavors of your pudding or custard with vanilla extract, cocoa powder, or spices like cinnamon or nutmeg.

Optional Toppings: Consider adding fresh fruits, toasted nuts, coconut flakes, or a dusting of cocoa powder as optional toppings to enhance the presentation and taste of your pudding or custard.

Section 16: Indulgent and Irresistible Plant-Based Cookies and Bars

Techniques:

Dough Preparation: Combine dry ingredients like flour, baking powder, and salt, then mix in wet ingredients such as plant-based butter or coconut oil, sweeteners, and flavorings to create a cookie or bar dough.

Shaping and Portioning: Shape the dough into individual cookies or press it into a baking dish for bar cookies, ensuring even thickness and consistent shape.

Baking and Cooling: Bake the cookies or bars until they are golden brown and cooked through, then allow them to cool completely before serving to achieve the desired texture.

Optional Additions: Customize your cookies and bars by incorporating ingredients like chocolate chips, nuts, dried fruits, or shredded coconut for added texture and flavor.

Handful of Ingredients:

Flour: Use all-purpose flour or a blend of all-purpose and whole wheat flour as the base for your plant-based cookies and bars.

Plant-Based Butter or Coconut Oil: Incorporate plant-based butter or solid coconut oil to provide richness and moisture to your cookie or bar dough.

Sweeteners: Choose natural sweeteners like maple syrup, coconut sugar, or date syrup to sweeten your cookies and bars without relying on refined sugars.

Flavorings: Enhance the flavor of your cookies and bars with ingredients like vanilla extract, almond extract, or spices such as cinnamon or ginger.

Optional Additions: Customize your cookies and bars by adding ingredients like chocolate chips, chopped nuts, dried fruits, shredded coconut, or seeds for additional texture and flavor.

From heavenly tarts and galettes to wholesome crumbles and cobblers, luxurious mousses and parfaits, decadent cheesecakes, and divine pies, this chapter has showcased a wide range of desserts that are not only delicious but also aligned with a plant-based lifestyle.

Throughout this chapter, we have explored various techniques and ingredients that allow us to recreate classic desserts using plant-based alternatives. From creating silky and smooth textures in mousse and custard-based desserts to achieving flaky and buttery crusts in pies and tarts, we have discovered that plant-based desserts can be just as indulgent, flavorful, and satisfying as their non-plant-based counterparts.

By utilizing plant-based ingredients like nuts, fruits, natural sweeteners, and dairy alternatives, we have shown that it is possible to create desserts that are not only delicious but also nourishing. We have embraced the creativity and versatility of plant-based ingredients, experimenting with flavors, textures, and techniques to create desserts that cater to our sweet cravings while honoring our commitment to a plant-based lifestyle.

In each section of this chapter, we have provided detailed information, techniques, and a handful of ingredients that allow you to embark on your own culinary journey. Whether you're an experienced dessert enthusiast or a novice in the kitchen, these recipes and tips will empower you to create impressive and satisfying plant-based desserts that will delight yourself and your loved ones.

Samin Lisa

As you explore the recipes in this chapter, we encourage you to embrace your creativity and personalize each dessert to your taste preferences. Feel free to experiment with different flavors, textures, and presentations, adding your own unique twist to each recipe. The possibilities are endless, and we hope that these desserts inspire you to embark on a delicious and rewarding plant-based dessert adventure.

Emerald Apron

You've got this!

"The Green Apron: Plant-Based Made Easy" has been a transformative journey into the world of plant-based cuisine, offering a comprehensive guide to adopting a healthy and sustainable lifestyle. Throughout this book, we have explored the benefits of plant-based eating, learned essential cooking techniques, discovered delicious recipes, and gained the expert knowledge and confidence to create distinctive and nourishing vegetarian meals.

In each chapter, we have delved into different aspects of plant-based cooking, from stocking our pantry with nutritious ingredients to mastering flavor profiles, incorporating plant-based proteins, and indulging in satisfying desserts. We have celebrated the abundance of nature's bounty, showcasing the diverse flavors and textures that plant-based ingredients offer.

This book is not just about recipes; it empowers us to reflect on the importance of conscious eating and the positive impact it can have on our health and the environment. We have the opportunity to make a difference, one meal at a time.

As you embark on your plant-based journey, remember that it is not about perfection but progress. Every small step toward plant-based eating is a small but important advance towards the future of food. Embrace the process, be open to new ingredients and experiences, and enjoy the incredible array of plant-based meals that await you.

"The Green Apron: Plant-Based Made Easy" is more than just a cookbook; it is a guide to living a vibrant and fulfilling life. It is an invitation to explore the incredible flavors and possibilities of plant-based cuisine, to nourish our bodies and our planet, and to make conscious choices that align with our values.

Emerald Apron

We hope this book has inspired you, empowered you, and filled your kitchen with the delicious aromas of plant-based cooking. May it continue to serve as a trusted companion on your journey to a healthier, more sustainable, and compassionate way of living. Remember, the power to make a positive change is in your hands. Let "The Green Apron" be your guide as you navigate the exciting world of plant-based eating.

www.ingramcontent.com/pod-product-compliance
Lightning Source LLC
Chambersburg PA
CBHW071153130726
47998CB00002B/496